BIRDSONG ON THE SEABED

ELENA SHVARTS was the most outstanding Russian poet of her generation, as well as a prose writer of distinction. Born in St Petersburg in 1948, she studied at the Leningrad Institute of Film, Music and Theatre. The daughter of a theatre literary manager, she earned her living translating plays for Leningrad's theatres. Her poems were published in *samizdat* and abroad from the late 60s, but her first Russian publication, *Circle*, did not appear until 1984. She went on to publish more than ten collections of poetry. A book of prose pieces, including short autobiographical fragments, *The Visible Side of Life*, appeared in 2003. She was awarded the Andrei Bely Literary Prize in 1979, and the Triumph Prize in 2003, an independent award for lifetime's achievement in the arts.

Bloodaxe has published two bilingual editions covering her earlier and later work, *'Paradise': Selected Poems* (1993) and *Birdsong on the Seabed* (2008), both of which are Poetry Book Society Recommended Translations. She had just completed a book on the Italian poet D'Annunzio at the time of her death from cancer in 2010. Sasha Dugdale's translation of *Birdsong on the Seabed* was shortlisted for both the Rossica Translation Prize and the Corneliu M. Popescu Award for European Poetry in Translation.

ELENA SHVARTS

BIRDSONG ON THE SEABED

translated by
SASHA DUGDALE

BLOODAXE BOOKS

ISBN: 978 1 85224 783 6

First published 2008 by
Bloodaxe Books Ltd,
Eastburn,
South Park,
Hexham,
Northumberland NE46 1BS.

This is a digital reprint of the 2008 edition.

www.bloodaxebooks.com
For further information about Bloodaxe titles
please visit our website and join our mailing list
or write to the above address for a catalogue

Supported by
ARTS COUNCIL
ENGLAND

Thanks are also due to Arts Council England
for a translation grant for this book.

Russian typesetting: Fred Macgregor.

Cover design: Neil Astley & Pamela Robertson-Pearce.

Содержание

Contents

A dance without legs

Bloodaxe published the first English-language collection of Shvarts' work, *'Paradise': Selected Poems* (translated by Michael Molnar, with additional translations by Catriona Kelly), in 1993. Since *'Paradise'* appeared, Elena Shvarts has published seven volumes of poetry and prose in Russian. She is, by any standards, a prolific poet, and the quality of her work and the distinctive nature of the recent poetry are such that there was a degree of urgency about translating it and opening it to a non-Russian readership.

This edition takes its name from her 1995 Russian collection, *Birdsong on the Seabed*. The selection enables the reader to chart the development of Shvarts' poetry and the poems' changing preoccupations. In choosing the poems I have looked for those which might resonate in English and might even make the perilous journey across into English poetry. Other poems I have translated for their importance in illuminating Shvarts' eccentric worldview. Many beautiful poems slipped the net, to my great sadness, and I have promised Shvarts and myself that I will return to them.

Elena Shvarts is a St Petersburg poet and the city occupies an important position in her poetics. Michael Molnar has eloquently described the relationship between poet and city in the foreword to *'Paradise'* and I recommend his introduction to anyone who does not know St Petersburg and its literary traditions. In fact St Petersburg is a major theme in poems from the first collection represented here, *Birdsong on the Seabed*, but less so in subsequent collections, and for this reason I will limit myself to a briefer description of some of the terms of reference for a 'St Petersburg poet'.

The term 'St Petersburg poet' denotes more than birthplace – it implies that the poet is engaging in dialogue with her literary predecessors: poets such as Pushkin, Akhmatova, Mandelstam, Blok or Brodsky; prose writers such as Gogol and Dostoyevsky. The poet writes within the great traditions of St Petersburg and is part of a continuing literary and cultural heritage. One of these traditions is a fertile and lasting mythology of place. St Petersburg is the 'invented' city, grafted onto the land by Peter the Great, and its marble and granite classicism stands in direct challenge to the chaos of the elements: bog and marsh, river and sea, floods and gales. Petersburg serves as a symbol for man's uneasy relationship with natural forces: constantly at the mercy of these forces and often at the brink of being overwhelmed. Pushkin's narrative poem *The*

Bronze Horseman. A Petersburg Tale, which stands at the forefront of St Petersburg literature, describes such an overwhelming natural force – the floods of 1824.

The city becomes, by extension, the literary scene for a struggle between chaos and order, dark and light, reason and madness. Culture, civilisation and sanity are portrayed as hanging on the edge of the abyss in works as diverse as Gogol's *Petersburg Stories*, Bely's *Petersburg* and Pushkin's *The Queen of Spades*. In poems such as 'In transparent Petropolis we will die, / Where Proserpine rules us...' Mandelstam conflates the city with classical history's archetypal perished city, Persepolis.

Shvarts' St Petersburg poetry lies within that tradition of destruction and apocalypse. Her poem 'The Dead are more in number' describes a world in which the lyrical voice is a transparent ghost, walking unseen on the riverbed. It opens:

> The dead of St Petersburg
> Cleave to the living like thin snow,
> Like tight fish to the spawning run
> They swim the back streets' upper flows...

In the poem coachmen, tailors, floor polishers, detectives – the stock characters of 19th-century St Petersburg literature and life – swim through her like little fish. Only she is not dead – death's 'lacerations' have proved a vaccine against the real thing. The following poem in this selection begins 'If you and I should think to die' and it is an elaborate and joyful suicide attempt, a vital farewell to St Petersburg's bloodless landmarks, windblown yards, honeycombed tenements and ghostly emptiness.

> Let me kiss you, ice-flown river
> Let me drop you, moon, to shatter
> In the waves. O earth of mine
> Wind-blown, many-homed thoroughfare,
> Goodbye!

In both poems the city represents death-in-life, from which only true death provides release. The river in the second poem causes death – and death is violent, despite the heady joyriding and the poem's dynamic ecstasy. The river is a 'cut-throat razor', a 'hungry trident' which rivets and weds its victims. In Shvarts' poetry, the Neva and its canals and streams, are a familiar, but brooding presence, full of 'slippery creatures' and poised for vicious attack like a beast of prey.

Animals venture rarely into the desolate mythical city landscape – their absence is a matter for hopelessness: the few sparrows are the city's sparse currency in 'You keep me in your folds...'. In 'Mouse' the listener thinks she hears a mouse running down Petersburg's Nevskii Prospect after the world has come to an end – but no, it is only the ghost of a mouse. When animals are present they form relationships of silent, passive attachment, like the ever-present fond cats. In 'The Little Girl and the Rat' the deathly pale prepubescent child with the rat on her shoulder represents an ancient and appolline poetic union. This poem could be read alongside 'Genius Loci (*Rositsa*)', in which girl and mouse might be the same being – one escapes the dying *shtetl*, the other remains, but their features are peculiarly inter-changeable: they both sit pale in the corners as the elderly couple go about their dying, and when the girl leaves, the mouse wraps straw around its head like a prayer shawl and waits on. Human and animal are broken and humbled, compared even to earthed-up root crops in 'The Little Girl and the Rat'. The exception to this animal passivity is the poet's internal bear of 'The Bear's Dream' who has had enough of 'shrinking and moaning' and will break out of the prison of her body, snapping her bones as he does so, and roaring.

'Memory's Sideways Glance' combines a number of potent literary myths. The poet as a child is playing on the banks of the Neva, when a boy throws a lump of coal at her head. There is a mysterious unexplained quality to the incident – it reminds the reader of the unprovoked attack on the tin soldier in Hans Christian Andersen's tale, in which the boy snatching up the soldier is merely the agent of a powerful malevolent force. In this poem too, the boy's action is quickly blamed on the river, an evil and terrifying presence, sharpening its sabres on the city's granite. But the attack does more than simply injure the child – it opens the poet's 'third eye', and knocks words into her temple. It symbolises, in other words, the 'birth' of the poet. 'Memory's Sideways Glance' refers explicitly to the great Pushkin poem 'The Prophet', in which a six-winged seraph comes to the poet in the wilderness, rips out his sinful tongue, cuts open his chest and puts a burning coal in place of his heart. Pushkin's poem ends with the angel's command to go forth and burn people's hearts with the word. In Shvarts' poem the river, evil and indolent, does the job of anointing the prophet and at the conclusion the Neva is sharpening its 'marble-silken sabres', as if for the poet's sacrifice. The two poems share an ambiguity about the poet's role, both emphasising that the transition from person to poet is violent and bloody, even murderous.

Loss of mind and reason is another strand in the St Petersburg

13

myth of destruction: the raging chaos without is often transformed into the chaos of insanity within. Pushkin's narrative poem *The Bronze Horseman* provides a good example: it has as its hero Evgenii, who dreams 'like a poet' and whose happiness and mental stability are destroyed by the flood. Evgenii is one of Russian literature's most pathetic heroes. The title, *The Bronze Horseman*, refers to a St Petersburg landmark, a statue of Peter the Great, showing the all-conquering ruler on a rearing horse, crushing the snake of opposition under his horse's hooves. In Pushkin's poem the horse and rider leave their granite plinth and chase Evgenii about the city. The poem ends with the discovery of his body on a small island in the Gulf of Finland (where the Neva meets the sea).

In Gogol's short story *Notes of a Madman* the St Petersburg hero remarks in his diary: 'And all this happens because people imagine that the human brain is located in the head – far from it. It is carried by the wind which comes from the Caspian Sea.' There are few more beautiful visual descriptions of the sensation of psychosis. I have quoted Gogol here because in Shvarts' poetry there are a number of instances of mind leaving body, and all have this same tone of rueful, yearning comedy and visual surrealism. This occurs most notably in the poem 'Mind in search of a Mind', which takes place on the shore of the Gulf of Finland, and is given a setting and a cast, in the manner of a playtext: lyric subjectivity is fragmented into dramatic plurality, and both Mind and Mindlessness are distinct characters. (It helps to know here that the Russian words for madness means literally 'leaving-one's-mind-ness' or 'without-one's-mind'.) In this poem an old-fashioned round brass diving helmet provokes a meditation on the mind and its relationship to its own bony vessel. Mind and skull are viewed in an absolutely detached way, alongside the diver's apparatus and the crowd, which appears like a billiard table of skulls from above. The poet implores the 'wise diver' to give her the heavy helmet, the 'clothes of reason' to weigh down her free-floating mind. Yet there is also the implication that this aerial, bodiless freedom is a natural and productive state. When 'mindlessness' slips away into sleep and the Cretan maze, the return of the conscious mind is connected not just with words which then shoot about the body, but also with the body's production of the 'dreaded white blood cells' – suggesting imminent illness, but also suggesting the checks and inhibitions of a figurative 'immunity' against diseased imaginings.

In 'Above the gulf's fingers, the plains and the flatlands...' the poet bids her eyes and her sight fly off into the sky, she sends them winging their way out to the open sea. But the moment of release comes at the end of the poem when she tells her eyes and her sight to keep going, even if they can't find her when they return. Her vision will be free of her fretted, mundane life. This poem is again geographically located in St Petersburg – the city-bound poet at the heart of the poem sends her sight off out into the Gulf of Finland, and it passes Strel'na, a palace and naval base clinging like a leech to the shore of the Gulf far beneath. Just as in Pushkin's *Bronze Horseman*, madness and fragmentation are kept to the city's limits: Pushkin's poor madman is carried out by the water to an island in the Gulf of Finland. Dissolution – freedom – lies beyond the granite constriction of the city.

Shvarts is a poet of fevered visionary experiences. She strives in many of her poems to communicate a moment of absolute fervour, ecstasy or inspiration, unlimited by the physical conditions of humanity. And she simultaneously makes claim to these moments as part of her very particular consciousness, or perhaps her mystic abilities. The poem 'Alchemical Dawn' ends with the words:

> My soul is the roundest glass retort
> Filled with the salt of all matter.
> Angel or devil: whatever it brings forth
> It was born to experience marvel.

In many of her poems the lyrical persona is in the grip of such a spiritual vision: the writing is tense, racing, elliptical and maintains the super-observant detachment of the fevered mind. The poems frequently feature such transcendental moments, the moments when the big finger points down out of the sky. And these moments have a Blakean subtle-vulgarity to them. I find myself visualising them, drawn in inks and boldly coloured:

> What torment living is
> On this Midsummer's night
> Better, to be a dark spirit
> And fly over fields in light.
> Better to shed all flesh
> And enter the dandelion
> And with a single breath
> Be scattered far and wide.

There is an accompanying supreme poetic confidence: we *will* follow her vision and be complicit in it. There is no room for cool analysis or doubt. As Shvarts creates new myths in her poems the reader is required to put faith in these myths, and the accumulating and dynamic religion they make.

It is impossible to examine Shvarts' poetry without considering faith and spirituality. (There is a story that Shvarts refused to let her poetry be published in the Soviet Union because the censors asked her to remove the word 'soul', and so she languished unpublished for many long years.) We are drawn to the question of religion not least because of the overt religious imagery: the numerous souls, angels, archangels, mentions of paradise and god, martyrs and icons in Shvarts' poetry. But what unites all this imagery is not an orthodox religious faith, but an all-consuming poetic faith. Much like Blake, the imagery is Old Testament, but the belief is in a spiritual pilgrimage and openness to myth and inspiration, which adheres to no particular orthodoxy. Sainthood is not reached by concentration on the "righteous" religious life, but by concentration on the poetic life and on the word. The poet, as we see in the poem 'Memory's Sideways Glance', is the chosen one, the martyr, and the suffering of the martyr is the spreading of the poetic word. Time and time again the act of poetry is connected with violence. In 'Solo on a White-Hot Trumpet' it is the violence of the girl Earth, who holds a wire to the poet's heels and sends an electrical charge up through the body – song, created by the earth, for the god to hear.

> How earth's love eats us out
> In its crawling climb,
> Its desire to seed song in the spine.
> From under the ground, from under the earth
> From darkness, can You hear it yet?
> My unbroken solo
> On the whitest, hottest trumpet?

And in 'Polestar in the House' the poet holds with her forehead the line which joins her to the Pole Star (the star here the God-figure and addressed with a capitalised 'You'), and staves off apocalypse with a feat of breathtaking concentration and unflinching stillness. The messianic self-belief might seem overbearing, but it is leavened everywhere with startling sharp imagery, self-irony and, above all, a lonely and rather austere dignity:

> When I fly over the dark waters
> When I sweep over the black trees
> I have nothing in my pockets
> But a tangle of tobacco and Russian poetry.
>
> ('When I fly over the dark waters...')

Shvarts' religiousness is determinedly set apart from orthodoxy and her world is peopled by the marginal, the forgotten and the despised – the dying old man, the injured fox, the 'Fool in Christ',

16

religion's cast-offs and eccentrics. She implies that the divine course runs stronger through these individual and peculiar souls. There is a strong tradition of 'Fools in Christ' in Russian Orthodox religion and society – I have written briefly on this in the notes to the poems – and in the narrative poem 'The March of the Fools on Kiev' Shvarts writes an anti-folktale about these eccentric rejects from worldly, sinful Moscow. Kiev is a significant destination for a pilgrim, but those Fools who don't fall victim to bandits or drink themselves to death *en route* are assimilated into the landscape: one becomes a tree, one is taken up by the moon, another disappears into the water, and some of the rest are incorporated into bread which is eaten by an unnamed 'foreigner' and 'wanderer'. In his blood they swim and speak in many different languages like the inhabitants of Babel. Shvarts makes of their fates a religious myth. A myth which bodes badly, like that of the Tower of Babel – at the end we learn that the 'elders' pray no longer for the world, but for God alone. With the disappearance of these odd pilgrims we have lost the right to grace, and to some quality of integrity the world might once have possessed.

'Grand Elegy on the Fifth Corner of the Earth' is a poem which I have included primarily for the light it sheds on Shvarts' worldview. It is a difficult poem in Russian, much is lost in translation, but it is a useful inclusion in this collection and says more than I could about the complexity of Shvarts' broad spirituality. In Russian the title of the poem is the Russian phrase 'four corners of the light' which translates as our phrase 'four corners of the world'. At the poem's heart is the suffering nature of existence. The four corners of light tug ceaselessly at the individual, and yet at the midpoint of the cross made between them lies a vacuum and an abyss which threatens to engulf man. The four symbols of the gospels, the Eagle, Lion, Ox and Angel stand at the four tugging corners, making the theme of Christian martyrdom explicit in this poem. There is no escape from the 'crucifixion', except in the featureless darkness outside faith. The poet spurns this, and so the only possible way is to abandon oneself to the suffering and be torn apart:

> I desire them all. And I hardly noticed when North
> Flew my head, and my legs darted off South.
> And I was torn in two, the chattering spring of my heart
> Now a quivering bush, bloodied and barbed in its place.
> And there we all are: racked and twisted and wrung...

Shvarts' more recent poetry includes poems written during a period in Rome. The Roman poems are almost all concerned with the spirit of the town, or, at least, some palpable universal and historical spirit, unique to Rome. The spirit is 'indifferent' to all that is not Rome, but in the case of the poet, it is actively malevolent. In Rome she has a rerun of the incident by the Neva when the boy threw a coal at her. This time it is a ball, and in her pain and confusion she hears the furies and serpents whispering to her not to walk over the place of the pyre where 'the saint' Giordano Bruno was burnt. Once more the nature of the poet as 'chosen one' is revealed by higher powers in an act of violence and rejection and Shvarts mockingly reinforces and guarantees the literary importance of this event with a footnote quotation from Montaigne.

Shvarts' imagery is always visceral and unsparing. The poems are unadorned and pared down to their vital organs and there is no sentimentality or earthly ego to muddy the clarity of her poetic vision. Perhaps most of all the reader is startled and excited by the eccentricity and novelty of the imagery. Happily Shvarts' peculiar imagination does translate, and her images do remain powerful in English, because of their very bold simplicity. Harder are the poems which describe visions. They throw up difficulties for the translator, because trust in the poet's vision must be sustained and a comparable visionary quality must be found in the English. But we have few visionaries in English poetry and those we have are eccentric and inimitable – that is the very nature of the poet-visionary. There is no "neutral" language the translator might appropriate to describe the heightened perception of otherworldliness, or the grandness of the visionary's claims. I have mentioned William Blake, and there are many points of comparison with Blake, yet Shvarts could not possibly be translated in the manner of an unorthodox 18th-century poet.

Another very particular difficulty in translating Shvarts lies in the issue of metre and form. Russian poetry on the whole adheres to a rigid form and structure, and 'St Petersburg poetry' in particular is often composed according to strict metrical rules. Shvarts' poetry stands out for its structural "oddness".

She has described her poetry as 'a dance without legs' – at once the patterning of a dance and yet the absence of the grounding, pattern-making feet, as the dance takes off into the air. In this her poetics match her thematic concerns. Many of her poems are concerned with the idea of flight – weightlessness, freedom and aerial perception. You might describe her structures, too, as eccentric – as the poem moves forward into the "vision", or the experience of the poem, the shape of the poem shifts alongside; it takes flight.

The poetic structure is propelled forward by its dynamic "core". But how does she achieve this effect? Shvarts, like most Russian poets, uses free verse sparingly. Few of the poems here are altogether free, most have echoes of regular metrical patterns. Most often the impression of 'taking flight' is created by deviation from metrical patterns, which destabilises those patterns without letting go of them entirely. In the poem 'Poetica – More Geometrico' the rigid geometrical impetus behind the poem (and poetry) is confounded by the lengthening lines, the changing number of feet, and the unstable shape of the stanzas – but the anapaestic measure remains basically in place. Often, as in this poem, strained-to-bursting lines reflect the gathering tension of a 'vision' or moment of breakthrough – the trimeter becomes a pentameter in the Russian text at the line 'But mad dogs of poems came racing on sleighs', before reverting back to its trimeter for the sober reflection on the poet's lonely suffering at the end of the poem:

> But my mind was clothed
> Darkness was stitched to my skin
> How hard the wind blows
> In the word's corner shrine.

In fact the effect is sustained by Shvarts' rhyming techniques. Shvarts makes use of Russian's rich rhyming possibilities, shunning the full end-rhyme in favour of pararhyme, half-rhyme and assonance, following rhyming patterns which simply peter out, or are transformed into other repeated sounds. In Russian, where rhyming is expected, it creates the real impression of a soul scratching for the words which will describe an experience, a poet making use of a living language, which grows its own tendrils and shoots of sound, sometimes repeating a noise over and over again like a bird, and sometimes reaching out for a new sound to follow a new experience, as if bored with what has already been. The poetry of Gerald Manley Hopkins comes to mind, for its very similar joyous irrepressible movement, and repeated birdcalls of sound. In Shvarts' poetry rhyming often sounds organic, an unplanned poetic growth. The clearest example of this is the title poem 'Bird Song on the Seabed', where the rhyming sounds, echoes and snatches of each other, are like the sounds of the water, through which the poet-bird makes its descent to the seabed.

In my translations I have attempted to stay as close as possible to the Russian form. As you will have noticed from the extract of 'Poetica – More Geometrico', it has not been possible to preserve the metre of the Russian exactly, but I have done my best to use a form in English which will at least echo the Russian cadence. I have followed Shvarts' rhyming patterns in the English, except in a few places where I have compensated with other rhymes won from the English. Shvarts' rhyme alternates between very subtle whisperings of sound, and Tsvetaevan drumbeats of rhyme and etymological playfulness. I have tried to recreate this in our slightly stiffer language and it struck me as I was working on this, that her poetry was, for poets, a useful addition to English-language poetry: it widens the field of existing possibilities in its lissom use of traditional form and its protean sound structures. The rapt and visionary nature of Shvarts' work is also a welcome novelty. There are few contemporary British poets who would dare write about the calling of poetry as Shvarts does, or the poet's heightened spirituality and suffering, or even faith in the word.

In 'Birdsong on the Seabed' the poet-bird sings of the land above to the cold-blooded and indifferent sea beasts, but none believe it. This marvellous, almost miraculous, poem fixes the fate of the prophet and the poet in Shvarts' world – to sing with unbearable beauty of another reality to those who are deaf or indifferent to your song.

> Is it worth singing where no one can hear,
> Unrolling trills on the bed?
> I am waiting for you, I lean from the boat –
> Bird, ascend to the depths.

SASHA DUGDALE

ACKNOWLEDGEMENTS

Translations from this selection have been published in *The Liberal*, *Modern Poetry in Translation*, *The Reader* and *The Wolf*. 'Memory's sideways glance' was awarded a translation prize by the Stephen Spender Memorial Trust.

I would like to thank David Constantine, Olivia McCannon, Maria Wiltshire and Mike Pushkin for their encouragement, help and advice. I am very grateful to Elena Shvarts for her help and generosity.

Elena Shvarts would like to thank Kirill Kozyrev for his help with the cover photograph by Boris Kudryakov.

BIRDSONG ON THE SEABED

Песня птицы на дне морском

Вертеп в Коломне

(на смерть Театра)

1

Там жарко было, ну а здесь в метели
Приплясывают зрители, в глазах –
Тот, кто лежит в скорлупке-колыбели
И Кто – в морозных небесах.

2

Завеса, бархатная в синь, наколдовала
Иль Вифлеема теплый зимний воздух –
Что золота дороже и сандала
Вола дыханье и навоза дух.

3

И пусть, как шут, я на себя в обиде
И Духа я не вижу своего,
Но на земле везде хочу я видеть –
Как слиты тварь и божество.

4

Пустая сцена – ты толкаешь вверх,
Бросаешь в дрожь, священна ты, алтарь.
Царей и всех блаженней на земле
Кто здесь – помазанник и царь.

5

И на кого прольется вдруг ознобом
Источник сил, или слюна Отца,
Кого и ангелы под руки водят,
Как дочь венчанного слепца.

6

Когда я по Фонтанке прохожу –
То чувствую в глазницах и у губ,
Как пыльная вдруг опустилась завесь,
Театра страшен мне зеленый труп.

The Christmas Mystery in Kolomna
(on the death of theatre)

1

It was too hot there, but here in snowfall
The audience jiggle and stamp – before their eyes
He who rests cradled in an eggshell
And He who waits in the chilly skies.

2

The night-blue curtain conjures a scene:
Bethlehem's warm winter scent –
The breath of the ox, the dung's sweet steam
More precious than gold or frankincense.

3

Even if I am at odds with myself
Like the Fool, and unseeing – my own Spirit lost
Yet I will behold in every place
The commingling of beast and god.

4

Empty stage, you bear all aloft –
Holy altar we tremble before.
Among us here – the anointed, the chosen
More blessed even than Princes or Lords.

5

And one here feels the source of all strength –
Or the spit of the Father – pour cold down the spine,
Another is led under the arms of angels
Like the daughter of the laurelled blind.

6

When I am out walking on Fontanka
I feel on my eyeballs and about my lips
How a curtain of dust drops without warning
How hideous the theatre's greening corpse

7

Его грызут метели в волчьи ночи,
И сердце в нем окостенело.
Никто уже не плачет, не пророчит.
(Я мертвых не люблю и мерзкого их тела).

8

Уносит ветром маски, рожи, тени,
Белила густо сыплются с небес,
Но – со стареющей Вселенной
Не сколупни румяна, бес.

9

Рождественский вертеп и крошечные ясли,
Шарманка дряхлая, как вымершая птица,
Поет в Коломне, в вымерзшей столице,
Серебряные звезды смотрят страстно
На муки легкие и крови роженицы.

октябрь 1989

7

Gnawed by night storms' lupine teeth
Its once beating heart in bone enmeshed
And nobody cries or prophesies
(I hate the dead and their stinking flesh)

8

The wind tears masks, characters, shades,
The sky's greasepaint slicks on the earth
But demons – don't peel the shell of rouge,
From the cheeks of the ageing universe.

9

The Christmas mystery and that tiny cradle,
A feeble barrel organ, like a bedraggled bird,
It sings in Kolomna in the half-frozen town
And the silvery stars in their passion look down
At the pain lightly borne, the new mother's blood.

October 1989

Мертвых больше

Петербургский погибший народ
Вьется мелким снежком средь живых,
Тесной рыбой на нерест плывет
По верхам переулков твоих.
Так погибель здесь всё превзошла –
Вот иду я по дну реки,
И скользят через ребра мои
Как пескарики – ямщики
И швеи, полотеры, шпики.
Вся изъедена ими, пробита,
Будто мелкое теплое сито.
Двое вдруг невидимок меня,
Как в балете, средь белого дня
Вознесут до второго окна,
Повер*тят*, да и бросят,
И никто не заметит – не спросит.
Этот воздух исхожен, истоптан,
Ткань залива порвалась – гляди,
Руки нищий греет мертвый
О судорогу в моей груди.
От стремительного огня
Можно лица их различать –
Что не надо и умирать –
Так ты, смерть, изъязвила меня!

1989

The Dead are more in number

The dead of St Petersburg
Cleave to the living like thin snow,
Like tight fish to the spawning run
They swim the back streets' upper flows –
Extinction has come to pass –
And so I walk the river's base
And slipping through my ribs
Like groundling fish, coachmen chase,
Tailors, floor-polishers, detectives.
I am all holes – they punch me through,
Like a warm fine sieve.
Then, without warning, ghostly creatures
From a corps-de-ballet bear me aloft
In brightest day, to the second window
Where I am hefted, from where I am tossed
And no one so much as turns or stops.
This air is trampled thin, worn through,
The Gulf's fabric is torn in two,
See. A dead pauper warms his hands
On the fever in my breast.
And in the shooting fire,
I can tell each and every face
Death, how you lacerate –
My wounds are such, I need not die.

1989

27

* * *

Если мы с тобою умереть надумаем – давай
Мы грузовичок угоним прямо в рай,
Прямо в золотистый старый дом,
Мы его угоним, уведем.
Править оба не умеем – ну и что ж,
Ведь струной дрожить дорога, будто нож.

Зажиганье включим – и вперед,
Грузовик запляшет, его затрясет.
На лету прощусь я с родной моей,
С этим тайным наворотом, с этим ворохом камней.
Если будет очень больно, если горе подожмет –
Можно и самим у смерти разорвать осклизлый рот.

Сфинкс, прощай, прощай, канава,
Крепость мертвая на вид,
С виселицы Каракозов
Прямо на руки летит.

Вы, сквозные, проходные,
Дворы, доходные дома,
Вы учили, вы вертели,
Как по комнатам ума.
Вы, облитые настоем
Из египетских гробниц,
И шаров воздушных гроздья
Пронеслись – из милых лиц.

О блаженный и мгновенный, и бензиновый полет!
Будто гусь летит и плачет – больше так не повезет.
Грузовик плеснется в воду,
Утюгом ко дну пойдет.
Невской бритвою холодной
Нити жизни перервет
И острогою голодной
Друг ко другу нас прибьет.

* * *

If you and I should think to die –
Why not? We'll nick a van and fly
Up to that shimmering golden house
We'll joyride into paradise.
Who cares if neither of us can drive –
The road hums like a string, quivers like a knife.

Start her up and off we go,
The van dances, judders so,
Up I fly and wave goodbye: my land, my home,
This coveted finery, this pile of stone!
And if it hurts, if grief overwhelms
We'll part the slimy lips of death ourselves.

Goodbye sphinx, goodbye canal
Goodbye fortress with your bloodless face
Karakozov flies free
Of the gallows, and into our embrace.

You, wind-blown thoroughfares,
Yards and houses of a thousand homes,
You taught me, twisting, turning
Like disembodied minds through rooms.
You, drenched in spirits
Distilled from Egyptian tombs,
And pleasant faces wafting past,
Like clustered blank balloons.

Oh this blithe and momentary petrol-fuelled ascent,
Like a weeping goose flying – the charm won't work again
The van tips into water
And sinks to the bed
And the Neva's cut-throat razor
Shears life's threads
And with its hungry trident
We are riveted and wed.

Поцелуемся с тобою, река ледоходная,
Разобьем тебя в воде, луна родная.
О прощай, моя земля доходная,
О сквозная, проходная!

Let me kiss you, ice-flown river
Let me drop you, moon, to shatter
In the waves. O earth of mine
Wind-blown, many-homed thoroughfare,
Goodbye!

* * *

По Солнцу путь держи, по Солнцу,
Хотя оно уже склонилось
К болотцу низкому – в оконцах,
Покрытых пленкой. Провалилось.
Легко пойдем и по Луне,
Во тьме играющим звездам
На барабане, когда оне
Идут под землю навстречу нам.
В час между Солнцем и Луной,
Между звездой и звездным хором,
Когда еще не пели птицы,
Но в ожиданьи дирижера –
Тогда вступаю на дорогу,
Где нет ни севера, ни юга,
Она ведет в селенья Бога,
И ангелы бредут оттуда.
Она как радуга висит
Через телесный злой овраг,
И в этот предрассветный миг
Я успеваю сделать шаг.

1992

* * *

Set your course by the Sun, the Sun
Although it has already slunk
Low to the marshy ground, the film-covered
Windows... And sunk.
But we may walk so light by the moon
The stars that play in the dusk
On a drum, as they move
Under the earth towards us.
In the single hour between sun and moon
Between star and choirs of stars
When the birds wait hushed,
For the conductor's words
Then I step out on the road,
Which leads neither South, nor North –
It leads to the dwellings of God
From where angels come forth
And hang like a rainbow
Over wicked bodily depths
And in this last moment of day
I manage a single step.

1992

Последняя ночь

Теснясь, толкаясь,
Звезды высыпали на работу,
Вымыты до боли, на парад.
Звезда хотела бы упасть – о что ты, что ты!
Сей ночью подержись, не падай, брат.
Сей ночью надо блеском изойти,
Сияньем проколоть глаза у мертвых,
Златиться в реках, на морском пути –
Сверкай, сияй, мерцай, коли –
В долинах, шахтах и аортах
В святую ночь – последнюю – Земли.

Заутра мы осыплемся, как прах, –
Беда живым, надежда в мертвецах.

Сосцы питающие, не питайте.
Ложесна, закрывайтесь, не рождайте.
Смотрите – звезды заплясали, как горох.
Шаги вы слышите? То не рассвет, а Бог.
Телец идет туда, где ждет Стрелец,
На атомы разбился Козий Рог,
Созвездий нет, гармонии конец.
Созвездий нет, есть сумасшедший снег
Из расплясавшихся звездинок, из огня,
Селена разломилась вдруг, звеня,
Но Жизнь еще жива – до утра дня.

Молитвы и стихи, в пустынях и столицах –
Играйте, пойте во всю мочь,
Живые, изживайте эту ночь,
Женитесь на деревьях, смейтесь с птицей.
Вам, силы Жизни, больше не помочь.

1990

The Last Night

Crowding, jostling
The stars stream out to work,
Painfully clean, on parade.
A star wants to fall – Pull yourself together!
Tonight you must hold out. No falling.
Tonight you must outshine yourselves,
Gouge out corpses' eyes with your shining
Gild the rivers, and on the seaways
Sparkle, shine, glimmer, gouge
In valleys, mines, aortas
On this holy night – the last – on Earth.

Come morning we will scatter like ashes –
Woe to the living, all hope lies in corpses.

Suckling nipples, flow no longer.
Womb be sealed, teem no longer.
See the stars are skipping like peas.
Those steps you hear, not dawn, but God.
Taurus moves to where Sagittarius awaits him,
Capricorn smashes to a thousand atoms,
The constellations are gone, harmony is over.
The constellations are gone. There is a mad snow
From the wild dancing stars, from the flames,
Selene suddenly snaps with a jingling,
But Life is still living, till the morning of day.

Prayers and poems in the deserts and cities
Play and sing with all your might,
The living must outlive this night,
Be wedded to trees, laugh with the bird.
Forces of Life, you are beyond help.

1990

35

Боковое зрение памяти

В оны дни
Играли мы в войну
На берегу Невы.
Восточный свежий ветер дул,
За белое пальто ее в залив тянул,
И я на это засмотрелась,
Когда мальчишка вдруг, ощерясь,
Метнул
Зазубренный угля кусок
В висок.
(Висок ведь по-английски – храм.)
И сразу кончилась игра.

А может быть, сама Нева
Ленивая приподнялась,
Мне вскрыла сбоку третий глаз
И заплескалась в головах.
О злая! – это ты, Нева,
И ладожская твоя сила
Тот уголь с берега схватила
И втерла мне в висок слова.
Кровь пролилась, ручьясь, ветвясь,
Сквозь антрацитовую грязь,
Смешались алость с бледнотой,
И угля перистая тень,
И голова была – закат
В короткий предвесенний день.

Горела долго над Невой
И вдруг, кружась, промчалась мимо,
Вся в клубах сигаретна дыма,
И мимо рук – седым углем
И лейкоцитом серафима.
Смотрела – как сестра летит,
Простая чёрная кость Адамля.
Нева точила о гранит
Свои муаровые сабли.

1985

Memory's sideways glance

Once upon a time
We were playing at war
On the bank of the river Neva.
It was blowing a fresh Easterly,
Dragging the river by her white coat to sea,
And I was lost in contemplation of this,
When suddenly a boy, grinding his teeth,
Hurled
A jagged lump of coal
At my temple
(Temple has two meanings in English).
And the game was over.

But perhaps it was the Neva herself
The indolent Neva lifted herself
Came to my side, opened my third eye
And took up lapping in our heads.
Oh evil! Evil you are, Neva
With your might from Ladoga –
You seized that coal from the bank
And knocked the words into my temple.
Blood poured in streams and tributaries
Through the anthracite grime,
Pallor mixed with crimson
And the plumed shadow of coal.
And my head was the sun setting
On that short day before spring.

It burnt for a time above the Neva
Then circled, suddenly darted,
Enshrouded in cigarette smoke
Past my hands like ashen coal,
Like a seraph's white corpuscle.
I saw a branch – a rib of Adam,
Charcoaled, flying like a sister.
The Neva whets on granite banks
Its marble-silken sabres.

1985

Poetica – more geometrico *

Паралелльные строки сошлись.
В их скрещенном углу закраснелся приют.
Уезжала с вокзальных лучей, что ведут
На все стороны – но слились
И все души мои столкнулись тут
И разбились о крепкую тьму,
Непостижную дальше уму.

Заблудилась в лесу, утонула в морях.
О душа, ты взывала из ямы ввысь,
Но стихи, как собаки, неслись в сумасшедших санях,
Параллельные тропы сошлись.

И сошлись они там, откуда ушли –
В этом остро-тупом углу,
Там ланцетом изъяли подкожную жизнь,
И живу я теперь, где они сошлись –
В каждой букве дрожит по углю.

Но одежду дали уму
На живое пришитую тьму,
Слишком сильно ветер шумит
В этом красном словесном углу.

февраль 1994

* Поэзия – геометрическим способом (с помощью геометрии).

Poetica – more geometrico *

Parallel lines intersected
A haven's red light in the angle created.
On railway beams I departed
That darted all over, but at last connected
And there, head-on, my souls collide
And are dashed and shattered about the side –
Of dense and unyielding dark.

I was lost in the wood, I drowned in the sea
O soul, you called from the pit to the stars
But mad dogs of poems came racing on sleighs
And parallel paths merged.

And they merged at their own point of departure
A crook, as obtuse as acute
Where the skin was lanced, the under-life drained
And now I abide at the place where they joined –
In every letter a coal throbs.

But my mind was clothed
Darkness was stitched to my skin
How hard the wind blows
In the word's corner shrine.

February 1994

* Poetry – as demonstrated by geometry.

39

* * *

Ты меня держишь в пазухах,
Город, таишь в углах,
Будто сверчка запечного
В складках своих и узлах,
В саже печей угасших,
В углях сгоревших дров,
В сотах домов доходных,
В крошках для воробьев.
Ты же мной и заплатишь,
Выгонишь из дверей –
Как воробьев не хватит,
Мелкой монеты твоей.

1994

* * *

You keep me in your folds,
Town, you hide me in your cracks,
Like the stove's singing cricket
In your dimples and your nooks,
In the soot of once-warm fires
In the charred remains of wood,
The honeycombs of rented rooms
And sparrows' crumbs of bread.
Use me as your currency
And chase me from the door –
But how few are the sparrows,
Those little coins of yours.

1994

* * *

Когда лечу над темною водой
И проношусь над черными лесами,
Нет у меня в карманах ничего –
Табак вразмешку с русскими стихами.

Когда же ангел душу понесет,
Ее обняв в тумане – и во пламя,
Нет тела у меня и нету слез,
А только торба в сердце со стихами.

Но прежде, чем влететь в распахнутый огонь:
Не жги – молю – оставь мне эту малость,
И ангел говорит: оставь ее, не тронь,
Она вся светлым ядом напиталась.

* * *

When I fly over the dark waters
When I sweep over the black trees
I have nothing in my pockets
But a tangle of tobacco and Russian poetry.

When an angel carries away my soul
All shrouded in fog, folded in flames
I have no body, no tears to weep
Just a bag in my heart, full of poems.

But before flying into the fire's wide mouth
I beg them: don't burn it. Leave me this crumb
And an angel speaks: stay away from her –
She is soaked in the brightest venom.

Круговрашение времени в теле

Эта девушка – чья-то дочь,
В глазах – голубая вода,
В паху у нее – глухая рваная ночь
И розовая звезда.

А в сердце у ней – который час?
Между собакой и волком.
Синий сумеречный льется атлас
Под воткнутой в центр иголкой.

А во лбу у нее предрассветный сад –
Занялось – вот сейчас рассветет,
Но в затылке уже багровый закат,
В позвоночник полночь ползет.

февраль 1995

The Circulation of Time in the Body

This girl is someone's daughter,
In her eyes the bluest water,
In her groin – the torn blank night
And a rosy star.

But what time is it in her heart?
Entre chien et loup.
Satin twilight pours its blue
Under the needle piercing it through.

And her forehead is a garden before dawn –
Look – dawn is breaking, the sun must rise.
But the back of her head is purple evening,
And midnight is crawling up her spine.

February 1995

* * *

Как стыдно стариться –
Не знаю почему,
Ведь я зарока не давала
Не уходить в ночную тьму,
Не ускользать во мрак подвала,
Себе сединами светя,
Я и себе не обещала,
Что буду вечное дитя.
Но все ж неловко мне невольно,
Всем увяданье очевидно.
Я знаю – почему так больно,
Но почему так стыдно, стыдно?

1994

* * *

How shameful it is to grow old –
I don't know why,
After all I never made a vow
I wouldn't die,
Or slip away, my white hairs shining
To the pitch dark cellar
Nor did I promise myself
I'd stay a child forever,
But all the same I'm suddenly uneasy –
My withering is plain.
I know why it hurts so much,
But why, oh why, this sense of shame?

1994

Девочка и крыса

Девочка шла с крысой на плече,
Крыса распласталась, как погон.
Этому никто не удивлялся,
Потому что это – древний сон.
Крыса живо-живо посмотрела,
Гладит девочка ей корнеплодный хвост,
А сама – серее, чем картошка,
Не пошла еще ни в цвет, ни в рост.
Снег их кроет сереньким пушком,
Удивляясь древности союза,
Крыса дышит в тонкое ушко –
(Но напрасно) – как немая Муза.

1994

The little girl and the rat

A girl walked out with a rat one day –
The rat sat splayed like a shoulder piece.
No one wondered in the least
Because this is the most ancient of dreams.
The rat darted looks, this way and that
The girl stroked the rat's hanging root
She herself greyer than an earthed-up tuber
Still without sproutings, buds or shoots
The snow, wondering at the ancient pair,
Cloaks them in soft grey down, bemused
And the rat blows in the ear's thin cup –
(But in vain) – like a wordless Muse.

1994

Заброшенная избушка

Печален старичок, допив настой на травке,
И думает коту, лежащему на лавке:

Ты знаешь, деточка, зверек пушистый,
Что вечер настает февральский, скорый, мглистый?

Что все давно недвижны, кто помнили о нас,
Забудем же и мы их в ночной и снежный час. –

Последняя чекушка допита, и теперь
Заклеена морозом, насмерть зальдела дверь,

И в окна льется синева, вразмешку с пеной.
Мы будем так лежать – и разомкнутся стены,

Покуда потолок на отворит нам путь,
По льдистой колее куда-нибудь,

Промерзлый домовой нас поцелует в лоб.
И сыплет снег не в гроб и не в сугроб.

1994

Abandoned Shack

The old man drinks his last drop and grieves
Thinks to his cat, lying on the seat

Know this, my child, sleekest of beasts,
This February evening will be twilit and fleet

And those who knew us are now long silent,
And we'll forget them in night's snow-quiet.

The last bottle is drunk, the door
Is dead-locked and sealed in hoar,

And foam-flecked blue pours in at the glass
And if we lie still, the walls must part

Until the roof reveals a track of ice
Leading us on to somewhere else

The shivering house spirit will kiss us at our wake
And scatter the snow – but not on our grave.

1994

Сон медведя

Я не хочу, чтоб мной играли силы,
Как на трубе.
Не буду я подсвистывать унылой
И мизерной судьбе.

С блаженной радостью встречаю
Я новый день,
Сладка сладка мне чашка чаю,
Утешна лень.

Какое счастье – что тебя
Никто не любит,
Твоих родимых во гробах
Засохли губы.

И вот летим – круглы и *о*стры,
Дробь из ружья,
Все растворились братья, сестры,
Ушли мужья.

И всё – от шляпы до ботинок –
Внутри пальто,
Переходя в раствор пылинок,
Благою стало пустотой.

Но что, на плечи налегая,
На лапах привстает?
Во мне, в берлоге одичалой,
Медведь живет.

Вся жизнь – зима, и он зимой
Все плачет, уменьшаясь в росте,
Но миг настал – и он тобой
Выходит в мир, ломая кости.

И вот весной – ау – весной,
Как время петь,
Глаза вращая – он со мной
Давай реветь.

осень 1994

The Bear's Dream

I won't have strange forces write me
Like a slate.
I won't whistle to the humbled tune
Of fate.

I meet every new day with blessed
Happiness
Sweet comfort, this cup of tea,
My idleness.

A blessing too, that you are loved
By none
Your closest lie with withered lips
In tombs.

And on we fly – round, sharp
Shot from a gun
Brothers, sisters, dissolve, vanish
Husbands gone.

And all of it, boot to hat –
Coat-stuffing
Becomes dust suspended
Merciful nothing

But who rests a paw on my shoulders,
Lifts himself?
In me, in this wild den,
A bear dwells.

All life is winter, and in winter
He shrinks and moans
But the moment comes and he wears
You into the world, breaking bones

And now in spring – hey, spring –
The singing thaw
Darting looks – he is with me –
And we shall roar.

Autumn 1994

53

* * *

Кошка прижалась – будто спит –
И тихо в усы поет,
И слышит, как сердце мое спешит
Как время мое идет.
Привычно земля, как грузовик,
Вошла в лихой разворот,
Травы очнулись под твердой корой,
Спи – еще солнцеворот,
Спи еще – сколько крови шуметь
В домашних своих родных конусах,
Знает дыханье и сонный медведь –
Сколько снегу скользить в часах.

1994

* * *

Cat presses close, as if she were sleeping
And murmurs a whiskery song,
And listens to my heart racing,
My time rushing on.
The earth turns, as it's used to turn,
Like a truck, on a prayer and a dime
The grass waking under hard skin,
Yet sleep – the sun arcs again,
Sleep – how much has the blood left to course
In these sheltering cones of flesh,
As much as snow, still to slip through the glass –
And that knows the wintering bear, and one's breath.

1994

Genius Loci
(Росица)

Белоруссия. Пустошь. Недалеко от границы.
Здесь было когда-то местечко,
Но оно улетело, как птица,
Все в нем шило, шипело, болело,
Но… немцы, время и ветер.
Ивы, полынь, ковыль.
Жила здесь бедная мышь
В развалинах нищего дома.
Она была здесь тогда,
Когда два старика умирали,
А в углу белела девчонка –
Отпрыск их ветхого лона.
Мышь белела в другом углу
И смотрела в дитя из-под век,
Девчонка шептала, молчала,
А потом убежала навек.
В солому закутав голову,
Как в молитвенной шали,
Мышь у камня сидит и ждет холодов
И сводит на груди концы печали.
Луна ей жует затылок,
Жжет проплешину лунный взгляд –
Вставай же, мышь, подымайся
И встраивайся в парад,
В котором идут, приплясывая,
До края земли – и раз…
А пустошь – она останется,
И золоченый глаз,
А мышке везде достанется
Черствая корка и лаз.

1992

Genius Loci
(Rositsa)

Belarus. A wasteland. Not far from the border.
There was a little town here, in this place
But, like a bird, it took to its wings,
Everything it held stitched, spluttered, ached,
But then came... Germans, seasons, wind
Willows, wormwood, long steppe grass.
A poor little mouse lived here once
In the ruins of a pauper's shack.
That little mouse lived here when
An elderly couple went about dying
And a little girl sat pale in the corner
The offspring of their ancient loins.
The mouse sat pale in the other corner
And looked at the child through half-closed lids
The little girl whispered, sat silent
And then ran away for good.
Wrapping its head in straw
As if in a prayer shawl,
The mouse sat on the hearth, and waited for frost
Made the ends of its misery meet on its breast.
The moon chewed at the nape of her neck,
The moon's gaze scorched her fur –
Lift yourself, mouse, stand tall
Join in the procession
They come jaunting, half-dancing past
And on to the end of the earth... and over.
But the wasteland – the wasteland is still there,
And the eye of gold,
Still, a mouse may find anywhere
A crust of bread and a hole.

1992

Мышь

Мир кончился: всхлип, вздох,
Тишь –
Но еще после всего
Пробегает мышь.
Гул отдаленных труб,
Вой уже близок,
По Невскому мышь бежит –
Нет, уже ее призрак.

Mouse

The world is over: a sob, a sigh,
Hush –
But still there is the scuttling
Of a mouse.
The roar of far-off pipes,
A howling, now close,
A mouse runs along Nevskii –
But no, it is only her ghost.

Предвещание Люциферу

*Господине Люцифере, если бы я вам гадала, то вот
ваша судьба – до времени и когда времени уже не будет.*

В тулове темной бездны
Кружился Крест ледяной,
Грубый, глухой, зеленый,
Как рубленый топором.

      В пронзенное перекрестье,
      В разверзнувшуюся рану,
      Влетали светлые птицы,
      А выпорхнули – мухи,

Сдирая на лету
Белейшие одежды,
В черном гнусном теле
Навзрыд они летели,

      А главный их водитель,
      Архистратиг и мститель,
      Косил во гневе – вверх.

Он знал – начнется Время,
Подымется Земля.
Потом придет Спаситель,
Оплачет Он ее,

      Потом свернется Время,
      И молот-крест расколет
      Земли гнилой орех.

Он знал – и до паденья
Он – злейшее из злейших,
Седой отец греха,
Что ледяное солнце
На плечи упадет
И станет, расколовшись,
Крестом промерзлым грубым,
Пригнет его к себе.

Lucifer Foretold

Lord Lucifer, if I were to foretell your future, then this
would be your fate – for all time and what lies beyond time.

In a body of depthless dark
Circled the frozen cross
Deaf, coarse, green
Like mutilated flesh.

Into the pierced crossroads
Into the gaping wound
Darted the bright birds
And out stuttered flies.

Ripping their white robes
From them as they flew
In the foul dark body
Surging forth like tears

And their leader
Arch-strategist, avenger
Casts angry glances up.

He knew – Time would begin
The Earth would rise.
And there would come a Saviour
To pay Earth's dues.

Then Time will fold itself small
And the cross-hammer's blow
Will split Earth's rotten nut.

He knew – even before the fall
He, the wickedest of all,
The grey father of sin.
That a sun of ice
Would fall onto his shoulders
And shattering, become
The coarse and ice-bound cross,
He bends it to his form.

Пронижет его ужас,
И ледяную душу
Прожжет чужой мороз

И с головой висящей
Из снежного Креста
Он понесется бездной
К источнику Огня.

Чрез Крест он продерется
В игольное ушко
И, ободравши плечи,
Смиренно упадет

Перед престолом Божьим.
И черный Огнь на белом
Начертит приговор.

1995

Horror runs through him
And his rimy soul is burnt
Through by another's frost.

And with head hanging
From the snowy Cross
He flees the depths
For the Fire's source.

Through the Cross he forces himself
Into the needle's eye
And, with skinned shoulders,
He falls in humility

Before the throne of God.
Where, written in black Fire,
Across white: his sentence appears.

1995

Песня птицы на дне морском

Мне нынче очень грустно,
Мне грустно до зевоты –
До утопанья в сон.
Плавны водовороты,
О, не противься морю,
Луне, воде и горю,
Кружась, я упадаю
В заросший тиной склон,
В замшелых колоколен
Глухой немирный звон.

Птица скользит под волнами,
Гнет их с усильем крылами.

Среди камней лощеных
Ушные завитки
Ракушек навощенных,
И водоросль змеится,
Тритон плывет над ними,
С трудом крадется птица,
Толкаясь в дно крылами,
Не вить гнездо на камне,
Не, рыбы, жить меж вами,

А петь глубинам, глыбам
В морской ночной содом
Глухим придонным рыбам
О звездах над прудом,
О древней коже дуба
И об огне свечном,

И о пещных огнях,
Негаснущих лампадках,
О пыли мотыльков,
Об их тревоге краткой,
О выжженных костях.

Птица скользит под водами,
Гнет их с усильем крылами.

Birdsong on the Seabed

These days I am so very sad
Sad to the point of yawning –
Drowning down in dream.
Whirlpools softly spinning,
Oh, give in to the sea
To the moon, the water, the grief
Circling, I am falling
To the algae-blanketed seam
The muffled war-like ring
Of bells draped in weed.

Bird slides under the waves
Bends them by force of its wings

Amongst the glowing of stones
The ear-lobate curling
The waxy husk of shells
And the weed-serpent unfurling
Triton is swimming through,
Bird takes pains to hide
Wing-shovelling down
No nest-building on stone
Fish, no life amongst you,

But singing to the bed, to the boulder
In a watery Sodom-night
To the deafest fish of the deep
About the stars above streams,
The ancient skin of the oak,
About candlelight.

And about fire and brimstone
The *lampada*'s unending flame,
About the dust of moths
And brief moth-pain
And scorched moth-bone.

Bird slides under the waves
Bends them by force of its wings.

Выест зрачок твой синяя соль,
Боль тебе клюв грызет,
Спой, вцепясь в костяное плечо,
Утопленнику про юдоль,
Где он зажигал свечу.

Птица скользит под водами,
Гнет их с усильем крылами.

Поет, как с ветки на рассвете,
О солнце и сиянье сада,
Но вести о жаре и свете
Прохладные не верят гады.
Поверит сумрачный конек –
Когда потонет в круглой шлюпке,
В ореховой сухой скорлупке
Пещерный тихий огонек –
Тогда поверит морской конек.

Стоит ли петь, где не слышит никто,
Трель выводить на дне?
С лодки свесясь, я жду тебя,
Птица, взлетай в глубине.

24 декабря 1994

The bruise-blue salt corrodes the eye
Pain pecks at the beak.
Sing, perched on the bony arm
Of a drowned man, sing
Of his life's path, a candle he once lit.

Bird slides under the waves
Bends them by force of its wings.

Bird sings as if from the branch at dusk:
The shining garden, the sun
But the cold-blooded beasts believe
None of the tales of heat, none
But the shadowy seahorse believes –
When a silent willow o wisp
In the little round boat of a nutshell
Falls to the depths of the sea,
Then the sea-foal believes.

Is it worth singing where no one can hear,
Unrolling trills on the bed?
I am waiting for you, I lean from the boat –
Bird, ascend to the depths.

24 December 1994

Поход юродивых на Киев

(Подлинное происшествие – см. Прыжова)

Злате Коцич

1 *Вступление*

В зло-веселой Москве, у кладбища, в ограде собрались
Юроды Христа ради.
Порешили они покаяться – и отправиться ко святым костям,
К пещерным мощам, что покоятся в граде Киевском.

Кто помрет по дороге –
Суждено уж так,
А, глядишь, доползет
Хоть какой дурак –
Пусть попросит Бога
О всех, о всех,
И отпустится
Даже смертный грех.
Безъязыкий пусть,
Пусть и хром, и сир,
Он помолится
За крещеный мир.

Порешили они – и отправились. Один уснули в кабаках,
Другие – в темных лесах, третьи петляли,
Вернулись домой, а иных – убили злые люди.

2 *Марфа*

Шла Марфушка, припевая,
От трактира до трактира
И, дорогу измеряя,
По стопушке выпивала,
Да и далее по тракту
На одной ноге скакала.

The March of the Fools on Kiev
(a real happening – see Prizhov)

To Zlata Kotsich

1 *Prelude*

In singlorious Moscow, within a graveyard's walls
Gathered a group of those who were for Christ's sake fools
And set their thoughts on atonement, and their sights on the holy
        bones:
Kiev's Monastery of Caves, where the relics found their home.

Some will die by the roadside
That is how it shall be,
But another fool will make his way
On all fours, if need be
And he shall intercede
With the Lord for every man
And he shall win forgiveness
For mortal sin.
Even a tongue-less fool
A cripple, unsired
May raise up a prayer
For the whole Christian world.

So they set their thoughts and their sights on Kiev. Some were left
sleeping in taverns,
Some in the dark woods, some looped
Their way home, and others were killed by wicked folk.

2 *Marfa*

Marfushka, singing, walked
From one inn to the next
And measured out the road
In cups and sips,
And hopped on her way
On her one good leg.

69

Вот Владимир позади,
И Рязань прошла,
И Калуга пролетела –
Киева не видно.
Хоть бы он из-за угла,
Что ли, выскочил,
Из-за леса синего
Выпорхнул.

– Поплыву-ка рекой,
Водой лучше я,
То болотом, то стручей,
То волокушею.
Выменяла злат-платок
На дощаночку-челнок,
Парус ставила – лопух наискосок,
И плыла рекою синею,
Баламутя облака веслом
Под корягой с тиною.

За ней рыбы шли
На хвостах, хвостах,
На хвостатищах,
Лодку мордами толкали до утра,
Говорили: прыгай к нам,
Мати будешь пескарям,
Осетру – сестра.
Пляшут с ней водовороты
И поет вода,
И никто ее не видел
Боле никогда.

3 *Лунный юрод*

В Киев ко святым мощам
Юрод бредет с клюкою,
Но что этот Киев такое
И где он – не знает сам.

Он разум на лучине сжег,
Пепел скормил траве –

Long past Vladimir
Ryazan is left
With Kaluga, now behind her
But still no Kiev.
Jump up on her –
If only it could!
Come fluttering out
Of the deep dark wood.

I'll cross the river blue
Over the water, onward
By marsh or by stream
By cart through the ford
So she gave her golden cloak
For a little wooden boat
And her slanted sail was a burdock leaf
And she crossed the river wide
Oars shivering the clouded sky
Under snag and river slime.

The little fish all followed her
Dancing on their tails
Until dawn they pushed her boat along
With their fishy kisses
And sang: jump in with us
Be a mother to the groundlings
And a sister to the sturgeon
And they waltzed the whirlpool with her
And the water sang
And no one ever saw
Marfushka again.

3 *The Lunatick Fool*

Towards Kiev and the holiest bones
Strays a lunatick, holding a staff
Hardly knowing what it is, this Kiev
Or where he himself roams.

His reason scorched bare on kindling
The ash feeds the grass

71

Только в круглой его голове
Тлеет еще уголек.

Пред ним вся белая, в пыли,
Луна бочонком катится,
А утром его по лесу вели
Бормочущие птицы.

Однажды он Луну догнал
И нечаянно внутрь ступил,
Как будто там Киев небесный сиял,
И с нею на небо взлетел.

Несет он посох и суму,
Кружится его житие,
Я вижу его, как всмотрюся в Луну;
Как белка он крутит ее.

О как одичился Луницы лик
С тех пор, как он в ней бежит,
Ума сгоревшего уголек
Личину ее темнит.

4 *Матрена-предводительница*

Топ – могучая Матрена –
Топ-топ – кряхтит, идет,
Переваливаясь, бредет –
Где же, где же великий Киев?
Кругом одни леса.

С пути свернула в лес дремучий,
Лбом в дерево – а там –
Стала грозовою тучей
С выпушкою по краям.

Стала, стала Божьим страхом,
Налетит в дороге
Прямо в душу черной тушей,
Вынешь смертную рубаху –
Вспомнишь и о Боге.

And in his moon-round head
Only the faintest smouldering.

Before him, all in dust, and white
Rolls the cask-like moon.
And after dawn the murmuring birds
Lead him through the woods.

Just once he caught the moon up
And found himself inside
As if heavenly Kiev shone there
It bore him up to the skies.

He carries his pouch and staff with him –
His circling saintly life –
I see him whenever I stare at the moon
He turns her wheel like a mouse

And how wild the moon's face grows
Since he wheeled within
The faintest smouldering of his mind
Has made her mask quite dim.

4 *Matrena the Leader of Them All*

Clop, the matron Matrena
Clop, clop, her creaking gait
Her waddling and wandering
Where is it then, this great Kiev?
Forest all about.

She turned into the drowsing wood
Leant her head against the bark
And there became a storm-cloud
With fur stitched to its skirt.

She became the fear of God
She swoops above the road
And into the soul, blackest hulk,
When you bring out death's clean shirt –
Then you'll remember God.

5 *Пахом-дом*

Вот пьяница бредет Пахом
В блевотине своей, как в злобе,
Идет молиться он – грехом
Бо он дитя угробил.

Все тяжелей бредет Пахом,
Вот позади уж полпути,
Вдруг стал он на дороге Дом,
Прохожему не обойти.

Едва войдет и соль найдет,
На печке вспялится сова,
А из-под лавки подмигнет
Ему кабанья голова.

Под паутиною висит
Вся темная икона,
А если бросится он спать –
Змея ему не лоно.

И стены странно задрожат,
Из подпола несется чад
Горелых тел – там двери в ад,
Там мучают убогих.

Из дома кинешься бежать
До первого в потемках стога,
От ужаса теряя тело
И превращаясь быстро в Бога.

6 *Лабиринт*

Вот Матрена потерялась
На лугу, на лугу,
Мы бежали, восклицали:
Угу-гуй, угу-гу.
Только след мы отыскали,
Только хлеб мы обретали,
Что Девица потеряла на бегу.

5 *The House of Pakhom*

Pakhom, piss-head, wanders in
Clothed in sick and spittle and spite
Whispering prayers, his prayers a sin
For he has ended a child's life.

Pakhom wanders, slurring, slower –
Half the road to Kiev now passed.
A moment's metamorphic power:
And he stands, a house, to block the path.

The passer-by is forced inside
The salt is barely found, an owl
Rises from the stove, the eye
Of a boar's head winking from the ground.

A blackened icon hangs beneath
A thick spider's web
And if he thinks to take a rest
A snake curls on the bed.

The walls quiver so strangely
The floor is a fuming well
The bodies of the wretched burn beneath:
Here the gates of hell.

So run and run as far as you can
To the first haystack, through the night
Your body dissolves in trembling
You become a God in your flight.

6 *Labyrinth*

Matrena is quite, quite lost
In the meadow green.
We called and called, we ran to find her
Hark away! and *Whither do you wander?*
Look, look, here's a crust!
The Maid passed by and in her haste
She dropped the bread behind her.

Вот глядим – лежит сухая корка хлеба,
Но, чудесная, растет,
Давит сок из ягод неба,
Подымает свод.

Мы на хлеб на той напали,
Стали грызть со всех концов,
Вдруг Матрену там отыщем,
С нею Киев и отцов.

Феодосий – он гундосый, он такой,
Он – безногий, красноглазый, он – плохой.
«Ах зачем, ах зачем я в краюху вбежал?
Как в болоте увяз, как в навозе застрял.

Мягкий хлеб, теплый хлеб,
Тесный пористый путь,
Я оглох, я ослеп,
Я теперь – кто-нибудь».

Вот Федула вбежала
С другого конца,
У ней нос набекрень,
Язвой рот в пол-лица.
И Пахом-живоглот,
И мордастый Максим,
Все вбежали во хлеб
И колышутся с ним.

Понеслись они все,
Кто безглаз, кто горбат,
Прямо к центру земли,
Как четверка мышат.
Как там сытно, тепло,
Не задохнутся там.
Жарский хлеб на крови
Со слезой пополам.

Они взад и вперед,
Они вниз – к небесам,
Нет Матрены нигде,
Закружилися там.

Dry old bread, lying in the grass...
But then the bread begins to swell
And grow, until it comes to press
And milk the sky and lift its shell.

We fell upon that crust of bread
We nibbled, chewed and carved it
What if we found Matrena inside?
And with her Kiev, and our Fathers.

Feodosiy, always honking, spitting green
Red-eyed, peg-legged, bad egg, he
Says, 'why o why did I choose this bit
I'm stuck in the bread-bog, like a boot in shit.

Soft bread, warm bread
Cosy yeasty dough
Deafens me and blinds me
Who I am now, I don't know...'

Fedula now, she ate her way
Through the other side,
Fedula's nose has lost its place
Her mouth a blemish on half her face.
And then there's Pakhom the sponge
And Max with the fat chops
All of them make inroads –
Around the bread they flock.

Rushing, rushing all of them
The hunchbacked, the one-eyed
To the centre of the earth
Four blind and naked mice.
It's nourishing, warming there:
They'll flourish and bud,
Breathe, and eat a pap of bread,
Made half of tears, half of blood.

They darted back and forth
And heavenwards – down
Matrena nowhere to be found
There they spun and spun round.

Тут прохожий прошел,
Странник некий чужой,
Он и съел этот хлеб
Пеклеванный и злой.

И четыре юрода
В его животах
Говорили на сто десяти
Языках.
И в его-то крови
Они вольно живут,
То ли он их несет,
Ноги в Киев несут.

Эпилог

Я шла, чертила угольком
По туче – что пристала?
И в страшный заходила дом,
Невидимою стала.

Но и невидимая я
Шептала и крестилась,
И долго в темноте рука,
Бледнея, все светилась.

Чужое сердце сразу стало,
Как будто кто отрезал бритвой,
И в нем сама себя шептала
Исусова молитва.

Пост-эпилог

Ты был там, путник? Ты прочел
Пергамент темный старцев строгих,
Что улием бессонных пчел
Уж не о мире молят, а о Боге.

1994

And then a passer-by
A foreigner, a wanderer
He took that bread and ate it
That fine bread, that wicked bread

And to his bellies
The four fools slunk
And spoke in a hundred
And ten different tongues
And in his blood
They are at liberty to swim
Is it him, then, carrying them –
Towards Kiev his legs bear him.

Epilogue

I was out marking in charcoal
A storm cloud – *leave me be*
When I entered a fearful house
And became a ghost unseen.

But this ghostly me
Whispered, made the sign of the cross.
And for a good while
My pale hand lit the darkness.

My heart at once a stranger
As if a blade had sliced it out
In it Christ's own prayer
Whispering to itself.

Post-epilogue

Were you there on the road with me?
You read the stern elders' dark scroll
That they pray like hives of sleepless bees
For God, and no longer for the world.

1994

SOLO ON A WHITE-HOT TRUMPET

Соло на раскаленной трубе

Маленькая ода к безнадежности

«Душа моя скорбит смертельно», –
Сказал он в Гефсиманской мгле.
Тоска вам сердце не сжимала?
И безнадежность не ворчала,
Как лев на раненом осле?
И душу боль не замещала?
Так вы не жили на земле.

Младенцы в чревесах тоскуют
О том, что перешли границу
Непоправимо, невозвратно –
Когда у них склубились лица.

А мытарь с каждого возьмет
Обол невыносимой боли –
Пожалте денежку за вход –
И вы увидите полет
Орла и моли.

Моцарта кости в земле кочуют,
Флейты звенят в тепличном стекле,
Они погибели не чуют,
Они не жили на земле.

A Short Ode to Hopelessness

'My soul grieves, even to death,'
He said in Gethsemane's dusk.
Was your heart never tight with yearning?
Did hopelessness never pace, growling
Like a lion about an injured ass,
Or pain stand where your soul should be?
Then you have never lived on earth.

Babies, yearning in the womb,
For the line, long crossed –
Irrevocable, irredeemable –
When their features were made fast.

The boatman takes from each of us
An *obol* of desperate hurt
Pay your coin at the door
And you will see the eagle soar
And the moth.

Mozart's bones roam in the earth,
Flutes sing under greenhouse glass
They have never learnt submission
They have never lived on earth.

Соло на раскаленной трубе

Под пятками разряды –
Красный ток кидает тело вверх,
Пробегая по жилам,
Зажигает фонарь головы.
Тут невесомых бабочек
Слетается толпа,
Они хотят огня поесть
И пламени испить.
Промерзлый островной маяк
Зрачком летит на полюс,
А волны говорят ему,
Таща его за пояс:
Ты знаешь – сколько лет Земля
Металась под деревьями?
Тяня к бегущим пяткам шнур,
Устала дева бедная.
Она копала из ядра
И грызла свою мантию,
Чтобы в неведомых морях
Дрожал, мерцал маяк.
Зачем же этот потный труд
Земли и ветхих жил?
Чтоб стая легких мотыльков
Сгорела в соль и пыль.
Жилы цокают, искрятся волоса…
Как пристальны к нам небеса!
Как рвутся в уши голоса!
Как изнурительна любовь
Земли – что хочет вверх ползти
И в позвонках песнь завести.
Из подземелья, из-под пола,
Из мрака – слышно ли Тебе
Мое без передышки соло
На раскаленной на трубе?

Solo on a White-Hot Trumpet

Electrical discharges under the heels
A red current jerks the body up
Runs through veins
Lights the head's lamp
And a flock of weightless butterflies
Comes clustering round,
Wanting to eat the fire
Wanting to drink of the flame.
Island lighthouse, chilled to the bone
Sends its eye's pupil to the pole
And the waves talk to it
Tugging it by the belt:
Do you know how long Earth
Has rolled under the trees?
Poor girl is tired, holding
A wire to running heels.
She has dug out the core
And nibbled her own mantle
So a lighthouse's trembling gaze
Might be cast on unmapped seas.
Why do the earth, these ancient veins
Toil and sweat?
That a flock of light moths
Might burn to dust and salt.
Veins hiss, hair sparks...
How intent the sky's regard
How voices clamour to fill the ear
How earth's love eats us out
In its crawling climb –
Desire to seed song in the spine.
From under the ground, from under the earth
From darkness, can You hear it yet?
My unbroken solo
On the whitest hottest trumpet?

Поминальная свеча

Я так люблю огонь,
Что я его целую,
Тянусь к нему рукой
И мою в нем лицо,
Раз духи нежные
Живут в нем, как в бутоне,
И тонких сил
Вокруг него кольцо.
Ведь это дом их,
Скорлупа, отрада,
А все другое
Слишком грубо им.

Я челку подожгла,
Ресницы опалила,
Мне показалось – ты
Трепещешь там в огне.
Ты хочешь, может быть,
Шепнуть словцо мне светом,
Трепещет огонек,
Но только тьма во мне.

Candle at a Wake

I love fire so
That I kiss it,
Reach out towards it
Wash my face in it,
Since the gentle spirits
Inhabit it, like a bud,
And a band of magic
Thinly rings it.
This is their home, you see,
Their shell, their comfort,
And everything else
Is too earthy for them.

I set my fringe alight,
I singed my eyebrows,
I thought... it was you
Flickering there in the flame.
Perhaps you wanted
To whisper a word of light,
The flame quivers,
But I am filled with dark.

WEST-EAST WIND

Западно-восточный ветер

Украинская флора

1) маки и мальвы в июне
2) подсолнечник в июле
3) конец лета

Маки украинской ночи
За селом залегли,
Как гайдамаки хохочут,
Черное сердце в сладимой пыли.

Черная бахрома,
Мрака темней, дрожит,
Сводит корни с ума,
Белый надрез их пьянит.

Мальва – она пресней –
Малороссийский просвирник,
Как украинская мова
Русской грубей и тесней.

Но она хлебцем пахнет.
Каждый голодный год
Пек ее, замерзая,
Со снытью мешая, народ.

Прабабушка младая
В венке из васильков
В омут глядит – Другая
Манит со дна рукой.

Врастают волосы в волны,
Чмокнет венок венком.
Вот под корягой Луною
Днепровский давится сом.

Ты, Украйна родная,
Потерянная страна,
Кровью меня согревая,
Манишь с речного дна.

Flora of the Ukraine

1) poppies and mallow in June
2) sunflowers in July
3) the end of summer

Poppies of the Ukrainian night
Have taken root beyond the huts
The *haidamaky* laughing, drunk,
Blackest heart of honeyed dust.

Black fringe
Trembling, darker than hell
Sends the roots wild,
The white sap makes them reel.

Their mallow, homelier –
Braveheart of Malo-Russia –
Is, like the local *mova*,
Plumper than Russian, harsher.

But has the smell of yeast,
And in the years of hunger
Huddled families baked their bread
Of mallow and ground elder.

A girl in a cornflower wreath –
My great grandmother
Looked in murky water, saw
Waving from the depths, another.

Waves and tresses mingle
The flower-wreaths embrace and suck.
And so the Dnieper sheat-fish
Is caught in the moon's snag.

You, my native Ukraine
You who are lost and drowned,
You warm me with your blood
And waving, lure me down.

Выпьет макитру горилки
Хитрый казак – а вдруг?
Товарищи мечут жребий,
Сбившись в круг.

И выпадает жребий,
И усмехнулся казак.
В глиняной люльке зарделся
Шелково-тленный мак.

Вот казак, накреняся,
Выскочил из шинка,
Гаркнул и повалился
В дебри подсолнечника.

А солнце вырыло ямку
(Оно ведь черней крота)
И упало в изнанку –
Где сумрак и нищета.

Подсолнух кротко поводит
Телячьей своей головой.
Семечек полное око
Никнет к полыни седой.

– Достань скорее занозы, –
Он просит у казака, –
Больно! Из налитого
Лаковой кровью зрачка.

Крот-сольнце, Луна – монисто
В маки галушки макают.
Гетман, канувший в Лету,
Плывет в свою хату на Канев.

Разве пестики-тычинки
Не просыпаны под тыном,
И сама на отлетела
У арбуза пуповина?

The cunning Cossack drinks
His fill of moonshine, calls
Full of daring to his mates
And they gather to pick straws.

And the lot is drawn.
And the Cossack sniggers
The poppy in its cradle-cup –
Corrupting silk smoulders.

A Cossack, bent double
Rushes from the bar and dives
Between the stalks of sunflower
Uttering a strangled cry.

And the sun dug out a pit
(Blacker than a mole, the sun)
And flipped round to its other side
Where all is dark and dereliction.

The sunflower gently waves
Its calf-like head, and droops
Its one round seeded eye
To touch the greying wormwood.

Finger out these splinters,
It begs the Cossack,
How it hurts! The great pupil
Throbs glossy black.

The mole-sun, the moon – a string of beads
Dipping dumplings in poppy seeds.
The Hetman who was dipped in Lethe
Swam back home to Kanev.

Aren't the stamen and pistils
Scattered down by the fence,
And didn't the melon loose itself,
Roll free from the plant?

Ты ли, мати Украина,
Плачешь в ивах, длинных, сивых,
И не ты ли пробежала
Под буреющей крапивой?

сентябрь 1996

Mother Ukraine, is that you,
Weeping in the ash-grey willows,
And was that you, running past
Where the nettles fade and wither?

September 1996

Арборейский собор

Душа моя вошла во храм
Ночной, презрев засов,
Она прошла через толпу
Рябин, берез, дубов.

Они стояли без корней
И трепетали в дрожь
И наклонялись вместе враз,
Как в непогоду рожь.

Как будто ветер в них шумел,
Как будто говорил,
То листья сыпались с ветвей –
Не дождь с шуршаньем лил.

И пред какою бы иконой
Душа не пала на колени –
Оттуда ветер ледяной
Провеял об пол чьи-то тени.

А на амвоне дуб стоял,
Кривыми крепкими руками
Он душу леса поднимал,
Как бы в лазурной чаше пламя.

В такт шепоту его и треску
Деревья никли головой.
И пахло лопнувшей корой,
Хвоею, желудем, смолой.

Душа моя тогда спросила
У деревца, что меньше всех:
Что привело вас, что свалило,
Что вы набились, как в ковчег?

– Конец Закону, все возможно:
Мы ходим, рыбы говорят,
И небо уж свернулось в свиток, –
Слетая, ахнул листопад.

1996

Arboreous Cathedral

My soul entered the cathedral of night
Although the bolts were drawn
And walked through the congregation
Of oak, birch and rowan.
They stood unrooted
Quickened in a quiver
And bowed down all at once
Like corn in gusting weather.
As if the wind blew through them
As if the wind muttered
The leaves were scattered from the branches
The rain stuttered.
And whatever icon the soul chose
To kneel before –
From it an icy wind skittered
Someone's shadow across the floor.
At the ambo an oak stood
And in his stocky gnarled embrace
He raised the spirits of the wood
As if a sky-blue cup of flame.
And in rhythm with his whisper, creaking
The trees bowed
And the scent was of bark breaking
Needles, moss, mould.
My soul then turned and asked
Of the smallest of those there:
What has brought you, why gather
And huddle in this ark here?
'All Order has passed. All
Shall come to be: fish speak,
Trees move. The sky unscrolls' –
So, scattering, sighed its leaves.

1996

* * *

Не переставай меня творить,
На гончарном круге закружи,
Я цветней и юрче становлюсь,
Чем сильней сжимает горло Жизнь.
Меня не уставай менять,
Не то сомнусь я смертью в ком,
А если дунешь в сердце мне –
Я радужным взойду стеклом
И в сени вышние Твои
Ворвусь кружащимся волчком.
Пускай творится этот мир,
Хоть и в субботу, на прощанье,
Встречь вдохновенью Твоему –
Опять в деревьях клокотанье.

* * *

Do not stop creating me
Turn me on your potter's wheel
Life's grasp upon my throat is tightened
And with it I grow quicker, brighter.
Do not tire of altering me
Or death will crumple me to clay,
But if you blow into my heart
I will rise in opalescent glass
Stealing and spinning my way up
To your mansions, like a children's top.
Let the world go on becoming,
Even at the Sabbath parting,
Your inspiration still meets –
An answering shiver in the trees.

* * *

Над зыбью залива, над гладкой равниной,
Над хлябью и глубью и ввысь –
Летите вы, очи, лети, мое зренье,
Как будто от взмаха руки.
Лети над водою – то выше, то ниже,
Лети, а не можешь – скользи,
Чтоб я позабыла в усилье паренья
Себя и заботы свои.

Земля разрушенья, о ветхая Стрельна,
Умильно пиявкой лежит
Под левой рукою, у самого сердца,
У злой подгородной весны.

Летят мои очи, летит мое зренье
По волнам, по небу и ввысь.
Вон облако, видишь? Вон радуга – видишь?
И если меня не найдешь – как вернешься –
Ты дальше над морем лети.

1995

*   *   *

Above the gulf's fingers, the plains and the flatlands
The peaks and the troughs and the depths
Eyes take wing, sight ascend
As if I had cast you myself.
Fly above water, rising and falling,
Fly, and if you can't, slide,
And let me forget in the effort of gliding
My self and my own fretted life.

Land of destruction, ancient Strelna,
Leech-placid you cling
Under the arm and close to the heart
Of a bitter city-edge spring.

My eyes have wings, my sight ascends
Through waves, high places, beyond.
See that cloud over there? And the rainbow – look!
And if you can't find me, when you turn back –
Fly over the sea and on.

1995

Покупка елки

Маленькому лесу из 48 елок – с печалью

В елочном загончике я не выбираю,
Не хожу, прицениваясь, закусив губу.
Из толпы поверженных за лапу поднимаю,
Как себя когда-то, как судьбу.

Вот ее встряхнули, измерили ей рост.
Вот уже макушкой чертит среди звезд,
И пока несу ее быстро чрез метель –
Вся в младенца сонного обернулась ель.

И, благоуханную, ставят ее в крест,
И, мерцая, ночью шевелится в темени.
Сколько в плечи брошено мишуры и звезд,
Сколько познакомлено золота и зелени!

1996

Buying a Christmas Tree

To a copse of 48 firs – with sadness

I won't choose trees in that little roadside pen –
Biting my lip and wandering, eying up their shape.
I take mine by the paw from a heap of the prone
As I once picked up myself, and once – fate.

Its branches shaken free, measured against a post,
And now its tip traces patterns in the stars,
And whilst I carry it home in the driving snow
My little tree becomes a sleepy child.

And the sweet-scented thing is placed on a cross
Restless by night; faint shape in the dark
A cloak of stars and tinsel on its shoulders
A weight of gold on every greening branch.

1996

Алхимический рассвет

В духовной трезвости я провожу свой век,
В сиянье разума. Но часто я пьянею.
Летела птица и упала вдруг,
Холодный синий глаз висит над нею.
Нигредо пережив, душа проснулась,
И снова птица бьет крылами в стену,
Звенящим белым мраком разогрета.
Она – внутри, но в ней уже светлее.
Душа моя, округлая реторта,
И солью всех веществ она полна.
Что ни родит она: хоть ангела, хоть черта,
Она для опытов чудесных рождена.

1995

Alchemical Dawn

I pass my years in sober spirit,
The radiance of reason. Still sometimes I am drunk.
The sudden plummeting of the bird
A cold blue eye hangs above.
The soul survived its *nigredo* and woke
And the bird once again beats the glass with its wings,
Warmed by the pale and ringing smoke.
It is – inside, but now lighter within.
My soul is the roundest glass retort
Filled with the salt of all matter.
Angel or devil: whatever it brings forth
It was born to experience marvel.

1995

Троеручица в Никольском соборе

Синий футляр пресвятой Троеручицы,
Этот лазурный ковчег
В мокрую вату вёртко закручивал
Быстро темнеющий снег.

Все ж я Тебя полюбила невольно,
Это небесный был приворот,
Съежилось сердце, дернулось больно
И совершило, скрипя, поворот.

Если чего виноваты мы, грешные,
Ты уж прости,
Три своих рученьки темные нежные
В темя мое опусти.

Our Lady of the Three Hands in Nikolsky Cathedral

The blue case of the holy icon
This ark of baroque blue
Swaddled deftly in wet cotton
By the quick night fall of snow.

I fell in love against my will
With You – your net was cast
My heart contorts, my heart is wrenched
And, shuddering, held fast.

If we have sinned against You
You will forgive, I know.
Place your three dark hands
Gently on my brow.

Почему не все видят ангелов

Геннадию Комарову

Ангелы так быстро пролетают –
Глаз не успевает их понять.
Блеск мгновенный стену дня взрезает,
Тьма идет с иглою зашивать.

Вечность не долга. Мигнуло тенью
Что-то золотое вкось.
Я за ним. Ладонями глазными
Хлопнула. Поймала, удалось.

А если ты замрешь, вращаясь
На острие веретена –
То Вечность золотой пластинкой
Кружится. Взмах – ее цена.

И если ангел обезьяной
Сидит на ямочке плеча,
То нет плеча и нет печали,
Нет ангела – одна свеча.

1996

Why not everyone sees angels

To Gennadii Komarov

Angels pass so very quickly
The eye can barely keep up
A moment's blaze rips day's cloth
Darkness runs to sew it up.

Eternity is short. Fleeting shadow
A golden slant briefly passed
I follow – eye's palms clapping
Clapping. Got it. Mine, at last!

And if you hold your breath and turn
On the head of a pin –
Eternity's golden disc revolves –
The price – a sweeping wing.

And if an angel of the apes
Should rest upon your shoulder bone
There is no shoulder and no sorrow
No angel. Candlelight alone.

1996

* * *

Не ночь еще, еще ты не в могиле,
Но смерти уж кружат, как братья возле Фив.
Так откуси себе язык, пока ты в силе,
Умолкни, не договорив.

Последнюю из голубых жемчужин
Не взманивай из дали в близь,
Последнюю другим не высказивай тайну,
Себе не проговорись.

1996

* * *

Not night yet, no – and not in the grave
But deaths are circling like brothers around Thebes
So bite off your tongue whilst you can
Leave things unspoken, no more speech,

Nor yet summon out of nothing,
The last of the deep-blue pearls
Or tell another the very last secret
Without murmuring it first to yourself.

1996

Ум в поисках ума

Место действия: Разгар лета. Большой спортивный праздник на берегу залива. Прямо на песке – выставка водолазных костюмов. Среди них медный шар. Дети пытаются надеть его. Водолаз уходит под воду в чем-то скромном и грязном. Никто не ждет, что он появится снова.
Действующие лица: Ум, Безумие, Толпа зрителей, Медный шар.

Медный, круглый и блестящий
Шлем, глядя на Залив, под солнцем весь сиял,
И на канате водолаз в резине
Потертой в море ускользал.
Что значит – быть в уме?
О, этот круглый дом!
От шара красного глаза не отлипали.
Подобно как желток о скорлупе,
Мечтала голова о нем.

Вид сверху на толпу:
Большой бильярдный стол,
Где в лузу нет прохода.
О, не толкайтесь так –
Мы – море черепов,
Где должен быть один.
Дробиться – мания твоя, природа.

Ум там – где медь и шар
И где заклепанный туманный
Огромный глаз.
Одежду разума и дом ума
Отдай мне, мудрый водолаз.

Я без ума, о море, люди и сорные цветы, от вас,
Но безумье утонуло,
Но безумье ускользнуло
В лабиринты сна и Крита.
Снова ум – в уме умов.
Снова он готов
Для выработки страшных лейкоцитов –
Перебегающих из вены в вену – слов.

1996

Mind in search of a Mind

The action takes place at the height of summer. A large Festival of Sport on the shore of the Gulf of Finland. There on the sand, an exhibition of diving equipment and in its midst, a ball of brass. The children are trying to lift it onto their heads. A diver in a shabby diving outfit goes down under the water. Nobody expects him back. *Characters:* Mind, Mindlessness, Crowd of spectators, Brass ball.

Golden bright circle of a helmet
Gazing out to sea, glittered in the sun,
And a diver on a rope in a grubby
Wetsuit slipped into the Gulf.
What might it mean – to be in one's mind?
That roundhouse of a home
All eyes were glued to the burnished ball
And as the yolk dreams of its shell
So the head dreamed of this dome.

The aerial view of the crowd of spectators
Is a large billiard table
With its pockets tied.
Oh don't shove like that!
We are a sea of skulls
Where there should be a single skull.
Nature's passion – to splinter, divide.

The mind is with the brass and the ball
And the huge eye
Riveted, fogged over.
Give me the clothes of reason
The mind's home, wise diver.

I lost my mind over you – sea, spectators, shoreline flowers
But mindlessness drowned,
But mindlessness slipped off
Into the maze of sleep, and Crete.
And the mind once more, in its mind of minds.
Ready again
To produce more dreaded white blood cells
And words, shooting from vein to vein.

1996

Полярная звезда в доме

Если от Полярной опустить отвес –
Он окно мое разрежет пополам.
Я и днем посматриваю ввысь.
Ты одна горишь не по часам.

Разве же сердце вковано
Во флейтовый тонкий свет?
Разве на цепочке – тяжкая
Плоская – мой брегет?

Или ты вьешься по небу?
Вьюнок? Или ты змея?
Ты ведь соринка в глазнице,
Ты ведь чужая моя.

От головы до центра мира
Упёрлась ты в висячий нож,
Его держу я лбом – а дёрнусь –
Ты упадешь, ты все сожжешь.

1996

Polestar in the House

A plumb line dropped from the polestar
Would slice my window, top to sill.
I look up now and then in daytime,
I see you burning there at will.

And isn't my heart forged
To your thin light-flute?
And isn't my pocket watch
At the end of a chain's cold weight?

Do you creep across the night sky?
Bindweed? Or are you more snake?
You are the mote inside the eyeball
You are my own, and yet distinct.

From head to the earth's core
You set your course at the hanging knife
My forehead bears – and if I flinch
You fall, you fall, and scorch out life.

1996

Большая элегия на пятую сторону света

Как будто теченьем – все стороны света свело
К единственной точке – отколь на заре унесло.
Прощай, ворочайся с Востока и Запада вспять.
Пора. Возвратно вращайся – уж нечего боле гулять.
От Севера, с Юга – вращай поворотно весло.
Ты знаешь, не новость, что мир наш он – крест,
Четыре животных его охраняли окрест.
И вдруг они встали с насиженных мест –
И к точке центральной – как будто их что-то звало,
А там, на ничейной земле, открылася бездна-жерло.

С лавровишневого юга на черном сгустившемся льве
Ехала я по жестокой магнитной траве.
Там на полуночье – жар сладострастья и чад,
Там в аламбиках прозрачных багровое пламя растят.
Вдруг грохот и шум – впереди водопад.

Обняв, он тянул меня вглубь, куда тянет не всех,
А тех, кто, закрывши глаза, кидаются с крыши навек.
Но, сделав усилье, я прыгнула влево и вверх.
И это был Запад – где холод, усталость и грех.
При этом прыжке потеряла я память ночей,
Рубины и звезды, румянец и связку ключей.
А мельница крыльев вращалась, и вот уже я
На Севере в юрте, где правит в снегах голова.
Но снова скольжу я на тот же стол водяной
Со скатерью неостановимой, и книги несутся со мной.
Тогда на Восток я рванулась в последней надежде,
Где горы, покой, там боги в шафранной одежде.

Но сколько же ты ни вращайся на мельнице света сторон,
Есть два только выхода, первый: паденье и склон.
Другой – это выброс во внешнюю тьму,
Его я отвергну, там нечем кормиться Уму,
Там нет ни пристанищ, ни вех, ни оград.
О нет! Остается один водопад.

Grand Elegy on the Fifth Corner of the Earth

As if drawn in the flow – all the corners of the earth
Met in a single point – and were then borne back to the word.
Farewell. Now weave and wind your way back to East and West.
It is time to turn home, the time for merriment passed.
From the North and from the South, now turn the stroke of your oar.
You know, it is hardly news, that our world is a cross
Guarded at its points by four beasts, who at last
Stood and shook themselves from their long-held pose
And advanced to a central point, as if they had been called,
Where, in no-man's-land, the abyss – a depthless gorge.

I rode from the laurelled south on a lion, taking dark shape
All the while as I rode, over coarse magnetic plains.
And there at midnight's stroke, a fevered lust, a spell
And within the alembic's glass purple flames swelled.
And suddenly noise ahead – the roar of a waterfall.

I was embraced and pulled to the depths where not all
Are dragged – only those who leap, eyes closed, from a high floor
But I jumped aside and up with all my force.
And this was the West: cold and weary and flawed.
And I lost my night's memory as I gathered myself to leap
Rubies and stars, a ring of keys, blushed cheeks.
But the mill turns its wheel, and I find myself now
In the North, the realm of the head, a nomad's tent in the snow.
And now I slip again on the same watery table top,
The books flying with me, a ceaselessly moving cloth.
But once I hastened East, fleet with a single last hope
To the mountains and the peace, and gods in saffron robes.

Turn as much as you like on this mill – the corners of the globe,
There are only two ways out, and the first is the fall, the slope.
The second – throwing oneself into the darkness outside,
I spurn that way – there is nothing to nourish the Mind,
Nowhere to shelter or moor, no landmarks, no boundary walls.
But, oh! That leaves only the waterfall.

Та страшная точка, она – сердцевина Креста,
Где сердце как уголь, где боль, пустота.
Но это же сердце – грохочет там кровь –
Наводит надежду, что в гневе сокрыта любовь.

Прощай, моя мельница, света сторон колесо!
Меня уже тянет и тащит, я вас вспоминаю как сон.
Никто мне уже не вернет ни ключей, ни камней,
Ни имен, ни костей.
Я с искрою света в ладонях лечу среди ливня теней.
О ливень, о мельница, о водопад!
Мы смолоты в пепел и прахом осядем на дне.
Лев, ангел, орел и телец растворились во мне.
Но если успеешь еще оглянуться вверх, на исток –
Там стороны света кружатся, как черный цветок,
И если я искру с ладони своей проглочу –
То чудо случится – я вверх в сердцевину лечу.

Уже меня тянет обратный подъемный поток.
Как будто пропеллер, а в центре его – граммофон
(А музыку слышно с обеих сторон).
И вот вылетаю в рассветную радость, в арбузный Восток.
Я вспомню тотчас, что мир – это Крест,
Четыре животных его охраняют окрест,
А в центре там – сердце, оно все страшнее стучит.
Я вспомнила память, нашла золотые ключи.

Четыре животных к концам своих стран побежали.
Чтоб сразу за всеми успеть – распяться надо вначале.
Ангел над головой, лев красногрудый в ногах,
Двое других по бокам, на часах.
Лука, Иоанн, Марк и Матфей
В розовом сумраке сердца сошлись со связками книг.
Сердце, сердце, прозрей же скорей!
Сердце глазёнком косится на них.

У мысли есть крылья, она высоко возлетит,
У слова есть когти, оно их глубоко вонзит.
О, ярости лапа, о, светлого клюв исступленья!
Но ангел с Тельцом завещали нам жалость, смиренье.

That fearful spot is the beating heart of the Cross
Where the heart is a lump of coal; there pain and nothingness.
Even so a heart – the blood within it throbs
Carries with it the hope that in anger crouches love.

Goodbye, mill – the corners of the earth on a wheel.
I am pulled and torn adrift – and you are no more than a dream
And no one will return to me bones, and names,
And keys and stones.
With a spark between my palms I fly through a torrent of shades.
O torrent and turning millwheel! O cascade!
We are ground to ash and to dust, as sediment we fall
And in me dissolves angel and eagle and lion and bull.
But if you happen to glance up, up to the source above
There the corners of the earth circle like an ashen bud
And if I open my palm and lick up and swallow the spark
A miracle – I am borne up, I fly to the very heart.

And now an answering current, rising and tugging me free
Imagine it as a propeller, with a gramophone horn at its eye
And yes, there is music, I hear it from either side
And I am propelled up to dawn, chorus, the melon-pink East.
I remember at that instant, that the world is a cross
Guarded at its points by four beasts and last:
At its abyss a heart, more and more fearful its beat
I remembered then my memory, I found my ring of keys.

Four cantering beasts ran to the ends of their realm.
Crucifixion the only way to keep up with all of them.
An angel at your head; at your foot a red-breasted lion
And the others standing guard, one at either side.
Luke, Matthew, Mark and John, in the heart's twilight
Coming together, in their arms, bundles of books
Heart, heart, regain your sharp sight!
Heart-eye snaps open and shyly looks.

A thought has wings, it soars beyond reach,
A word has claws, it sinks them deep.
Oh, the anger of the paw, the bright beak of fury!
Yet the Angel and the Bull bequeath us peace and pity.

Я всех их желаю. И я не заметила – вдруг –
На Север летит голова, а ноги помчались на Юг.
Вот так разорвали меня. Где сердца бормочущий ключ –
Там мечется куст, он красен, колюч.
И там мы размолоты, свинчены, порваны все,
Но чтоб не заметили – время дается и дом.
Слетая, взлетая в дыму кровянисто-златом,
Над бездной летим и кружим в колесе.

В крещенскую ночь злые волки сидят у прорубной дыры.
Хвосты их примерзли, но волки следят за мерцаньем игры
Звезд, выплывающих снизу, глубокие видят миры.
Зоркие жалкие твари – не звери-цари.
Волки – то же, что мы, и кивают они: говори.
Мутят лапою воду, в которой горят их глаза
Пламенем хладным. Если это звезда, то ее исказила слеза.
В ней одной есть спасенье, на нее и смотри,
Пока Крест, расширяясь, раздирает тебя изнутри.

январь 1997

I desire them all. And I hardly noticed when North
Flew my head, and my legs darted off South.
And I was torn in two, the chattering spring of my heart
Now a quivering bush, bloodied and barbed in its place.
And there we all are: racked and twisted and wrung,
But to keep our minds from it, we are lent both time and home
And so rising and falling in thick blood-gilt fumes
Above the abyss we fly, and follow the wheel round.

On Twelfth Night wild wolves sit round an ice-hole.
Their tails are frozen stiff but they watch the glittering whorl
Of stars floating up to play, they see deep worlds.
Hardly kings of beasts, those pitiful sharp-eyed wolves,
Base creatures – just like us, and they nod as if to say, 'well?'
And paw at the water where their own eyes blaze
With a cold flame. If this is a star, then it's maimed by a tear.

There is one salvation in water: keep looking in
Until the Cross, extending slowly, tears your flesh from within.

January 1997

A WILD-SCRIPT OF RECENT TIMES

Дикопись последнего времени

Жареный англичанин в Москве

(Миг как сфера)

1

Пробил колокол к вечерне –
Смерти миг для Елисея.
Медленно венец из терний
Опустился на злодея.
Палачи, хоть с неохотой,
Привязали его к палке,
Развели огонь в палатах:
«Царь велел, гори, проклятый.
Видно, царь оголодал наш,
Хочет редкого жаркого,
Хочет каждый день инова,
Он на то и государь…»

2

Колокол вечерний длится.
В этот миг Адам, отец наш,
Скользнув по времени древу
(И душа еще нерожденная –
позднего сева петербургская птица –
по ветке напева), – смотрит внутрь – и дивится.
Во времени чужом нету прав у нас – немы,
Не говоря уж о том, что не мы.
Дух чужой мерцает в круглом флаконе,
И там пляшет бесенок – сын сатаны.

3

При конце заката, на острове – в пустыни
Молит Бога обо всех святой отшельник,
О немой и говорящей твари
И о мертвых, что молчат так громко.
«Кто бы в мире крест сей миг ни нес –
Дай немного от его мне доли».
Он хватает долю, как мурашка,
И бежит в убогую пещерку.

An Englishman Roasted in Moscow

(The moment's glass round)

1

The bell rang for vespers:
The moment of Elisaeus' death.
Slowly a crown of thorns
Is lowered on the criminal head.
Unwilling executioners
Fasten him to the stake
Fan the flames within the chambers:
'Burn, you wretch, the Tsar has spoke.
Our Tsar is hungering for sure,
An appetite for roasted morsel,
A constant need for new-fangled –
In truth it's why he rules us all...'

2

The vespers bell tolls on and on.
And at that moment our father Adam,
Slip-sliding down the tree of life
(And the soul, as yet unborn,
Of a Petersburg bird, wreathing in song
More recent branches), gazes in, struck dumb.
Our rights in foreign times are few, we – the voiceless;
Fewer still have those who are not yet become us.
Strange spirit, lambent in the flask's round,
A demon dancing – Satan's son.

3

At sunset's end on an island in a wilderness
A hermit-saint raises a prayer for all:
The dumb and the talking beasts
And the dead, who hold their tongues so loudly.
'Whosoever shall bear a cross at this instant
Let me take my part in it.'
He takes his share, and ant-like scuttles
Back to his bare cave dwelling.

А тому, кто в этот миг вертелся
Как перегоревшее жаркое,
Сон был послан – что во сне он жарим,
А проснется – радость-то какая!

4

Пробил колокол к вечерне.
Вздрогнул царь в постели, древний
Византийский список бросил
И, покряхтывая, встал.
Целый час уже, наверно,
С аглицким стеклом читал.
И устал – пора к вечерне.
В клетке у окна певец
Застонал и вдруг заохал,
Византийская парча
Передернулась сполохом.

– «Вы, там! Потише жарьте бусурмана,
Велю я жить ему до самого утра».
Как бы по Божьему веленью
Спускалась ярость на царя.
– «Не против плоти наши боренья,
Но пусть злобесный в плоти пострадает!
Когда б не матушка, не плоть,
За что и душку уколоть?» –
Хихикнул. Испугался – ну как бес
Мне в душу выползнем залез?
Нет, это страшный огнь небес.
Как по стене прорезалась черта
И через душу, через сердце – слева –
Шипящий раскаленный камень гнева –
В ночь бархатную живота.
И воздух, комната – все будто закипело,
И это Божие, не человечье дело.

5

Бояре, затворясь, бормочут: яда
Он не жалел для нас, и так ему и надо.
Колышет ветер крепких слов ботву,
А в корне их: пора, пора в Литву.

And a dream was sent to the man
Who tossed and turned like burnt meat,
In which it was only a nightmare, the slow broil
And when he awoke, he would wake to such joy.

4

The vespers bell rung.
The Tsar shuddered in his bed, flung
The ancient Byzantine scroll to the floor
And, limbs creaking, arose.
He must have been reading a whole hour
Through his English spectacles,
And tired now. Time for vespers.
In a cage by the window the songbird
Groans, suddenly moans
The scroll's fabric twists,
And agitated, turns.

'You, out there! Make quieter work of roasting
The foreigner. I want him alive till dawn.'
And fury descended upon the Tsar
As if God himself had cast it down.
'We have no fight with mortal form
But may the sinful flesh be barbed!
For if not through the flesh's coil
How may we cull the human soul?'
He sniggers. Takes fright. Has a demon
Worked its way into his soul's cocoon?
No, this is the terrible fire of heaven.
The burning trail across a wall,
Through the heart, to the left; to the left, through the soul,
The white heat of a rock of gall
Hissing into the dark softness of the maw.
And the air, and the room – all of it seemed to be boiling
And this was not man's work; this was the Lord's doing.

5

The Boyars, locking their doors, murmured, 'Spend
His poison on us, would he? This is well-earned.'
But the wind flutters the tough leaves of their words –
Make haste for the border, whisper the roots in the earth.

6

Где зори не слышно вечерней,
В избушке замшелой
Волхв вертит фигурку, на ней корона.
Он ей пронзает сердце восковое
И стона ждет, но не услышал стона.
Швыряет в кадку, где пасутся черви.
Еще не вычерпал всю бочку виночерпий
И царской жизни темное вино.
Еще он правит, и мантия еще струится с плеч,
Но проклят нами он давно,
Его заждались смерть и печь.

7

А там вдали – где остров Альбион,
Сестре Бомелия приснился страшный сон.

8

Шел снег во тьме. Из церкви слабо
Сквозило тихое томительное пенье.
Рыбарь вез мерзлых щук, и на ухабах
Они стучали, как поленья.

9

Когда же сняли головню еще живую
И, веки приоткрыв, она шепнула: «Oh, my Lord»,
То солнце глухо-красное скользнуло
Быстрей, чем можно, под московский лед.

Речь идет об английском враче Елисее Бомелии, который сперва
ревностно служил Грозному, изобретая яды для его врагов, а потом,
обвиненный в предательстве, был казнен тем мучительным способом,
о котором здесь говорится.

6

Beyond evensong's reach
In a moss-covered shack
A wizard lifts a little doll with a crown
And sticks it through its waxy heart
And waits – in vain he waits for a groan.
He tosses it into a barrel, where the worms feed.
The cupbearer's jar is not yet dry
Nor the dark wine of the Tsar's own life.
He rules on, his gown still streams from his shoulders
But he is long cursed by you and I
And death waits with fires that do not grow colder.

7

In the distance, on Albion's far hills
Bomelius' sister dreams of terrible ills.

8

Snow falls in the darkness. From a church
The faintest and most plaintive of songs;
A fisherman carts home his ice-thick catch
And the fish rattle like logs over uneven stones.

9

When they removed the still-living stump
It opened its eyes a little and whispered, Christ
And the block-red sun slipped faster then
Than is possible, under the Moscow ice.

The poem is concerned with the fate of the English doctor, Elisaeus
Bomelius. A favourite of Tsar Ivan, he made up poisons for his enemies.
Later he was accused of treachery and punished in the manner described
in the poem.

129

THE SCRIBE'S STAFF

Трость скорописца

Гоголь на Испанской лестнице

А Рим еще такое захолустье…
На Форуме еще пасутся козы
И маленькая обезьянка Чичи
Шарманку крутит, закатив глаза.
Здесь у подножья лестницы Испанской
Еще совсем недавно умер Китс.
Весенний день – и с улицы Счастливой
Какой-то длинноносый и сутулый
так весело заскачет по ступенькам,
Как птица королек иль гоголек.
Но временами косится на тень
На треугольную
И с торбой за плечами.
А в торбе души умерших лежат
И просятся на волю.
А господин вот этот треугольный
Каких-то лет почтенных, темных,
Каких-то лет совсем необозримых
Бежит, как веер, сбоку по ступенькам.
И не отстанет он до смерти, нет.
Навстречу подымается художник
И машет Buon giorno, Nicolà!
А тот в ответ небрежно улыбнется
И от кого-то сзади отмахнется.
А обезьянка маленькая Чичи
Так влажно смотрит, получив пятак.

Gogol on the Spanish Steps

And Rome is still the back of beyond...
The forum is still grazed by goats
And a tiny monkey by the name of Chi-chi
Frowning, turns a barrel organ's crank.
Here, at the foot of the Spanish Steps
Keats died not long ago.
A spring day, and from *via Felice*
A man with a stoop and a long nose
Skips down the steps with such joy
Like a goldcrest or a golden-eye.
Now and then he steals a sidelong glance
At the shadow's tricorn
With its bag over its shoulder.
And dead souls lying in the bag
Pleading to be let out.
But this tricorn, this man
Of respectable and shadowy age
Of limitless, boundless age
Runs sideways, fan-like, down the steps.
And oh, he will not relent until death.
An artist ascends towards him
And waves, *buon giorno, Nicolà!*
But he in answer only abruptly smiles
And brushes off someone behind.
The tiny monkey by the name of Chi-chi
Gazes moistly, a new coin in its hand.

Римская тетрадь

Ольге Мартыновой

Воспоминание о фреске фра Беато Анджелико «Крещение»
при виде головы Иоанна Крестителя в Риме

Роза серая упала и замкнула Иордан,
И с водой в руке зажатой прыгнул в небо Иоанн.
Таял над рекой рассветный легкий мокренький туман.
Иоанн сжимает руку будто уголь там, огонь,
И над Богом размыкает свою крепкую ладонь.
Будто цвет он поливает и невидимый цветок,
Кровь реки летит и льется чрез него, как водосток.
Расцветай же, расцветай же, мой Творец и Господин,
Ты сгорал в жару пустынном, я пришел и остудил.
Умывайся, освежайся, мой невидимый цветок,
Человек придет и срежет, потому что он жесток.
Ты просил воды у мира и вернул ее вином,
Кровью – надо человеку, потому что он жесток.
Но пролился же на Бога Иордановым дождем
Иоанн – и растворился, испарился как слова
И лежит в соборе римском смоляная голова,
Почерневши от смятенья, от длиннот календаря
Он лежит как lapis niger,
       твердо зная, что наступит тихо серая заря.
Я прочла в пустых глазницах, что мы мучимся не зря.
Солнце мокрое в тот вечер выжималось, не горя,
Будто губка и медуза. На мосту чрез Тибр в мути
Безнадежность и надежда дрались, слов не говоря,
Как разгневанные путти, два козла и два царя.

134

Rome Notebook

To Olga Martynova

On recalling the fresco 'The Baptism of Christ' by Fra Angelico
at the sight of the head of John the Baptist in Rome.

The grey rose fell and sealed the Jordan,
And John, whose hand gripped water, leapt into the sky.
Over the river rose the light mists of dawn.
John makes tight his hold, as if grasping coal, fire,
And opens his mighty palm over God himself.
As if watering a flower, or an invisible bud,
The river's blood flies, pouring gutter-stream through him
Come bud to flower, my Creator, my Lord,
You were burning in the desert, I came and cooled you.
Be cleansed and refreshed, my invisible bud,
Man will come and cut you down, for he is cruel.
You asked the world for water and gave it back as wine,
You must give in blood to man, for he is cruel.
But the waters of the Jordan rained down on God
John evaporated, dissolving like the words
And his pitchy head lies in Rome's vaults,
Darkened by confusion, by the calendar's longueurs.
He lies like *Lapis Niger*,
    Sure a quiet grey dawn will break.
I read in his gaping sockets, our suffering is not in vain.
That evening a watery sun wrung itself, unburning
Like a sponge, a medusa. On a murky Tiber bridge
Hopelessness and hope fought, without a word,
Like raging *puttis*, two goats, two emperors.

Площадь Мальтийских рыцарей в Риме

Хрустя, расцветает звезда Авентина
Над площадью Мальтийских рыцарей,
Что Пиранези когтем львиным
На теплом небе твердо выцарапал.
(А в это время бедный Павел
Гоняет обруч хворостиной,
Не зная, что уже мальтийцы
К ограде стеллы примостили.)
Факелы, урны, Медузы
Белеющие в полнолунье…
А под обрывом в кипарисах
Выпь плачет громко, безутешно.
Как будто бы Магистр Великий
В подбитом горностаем платье
Все ропщет в этих стонах долгих
О несмываемом проклятье.

Piazza of the Knights of Malta in Rome

The Aventine star opens with a rasp
Over the Piazza of the Knights of Malta
Marked out clearly in the warm sky
By Piranesi with a lion's claw.
(And at this time poor Pavel
Was whipping his hoop along,
Unaware the Maltese had already found
A home on the constellation's bounds.)
Torches, urns, Medusas
Glimmering white in the full moon...
But at the foot of the cliff, in the cypresses
The bittern, loud and plaintive, mourns.
As if it were the Grand Master
In his ermine-lined robe
Mumbling on through unceasing sobs
Of a curse no man can revoke.

Небо в Риме

Где то в небе мучат рыбу
И дрожит, хвостом бия.
От нее горит над Римом
Золотая чешуя.
Только в Риме плещут в небо
Раздвижное – из ведра,
Только в Риме смерть не дремлет,
Но не трогает зазря,
А лежит, как лаццарони,
У фонтана, на виду
И глядит, как злую рыбу
В синем мучают пруду

The Sky in Rome

Somewhere in the sky a fish is tormented
And it flickers, beating its tail.
From it, burning above Rome
A golden scale.
It is only in Rome they splash the sky
Ever expanding – from a pail.
Only in Rome does death not sleep
Nor touch to no avail,
It lies like *lazzaroni*
By the fountain, on view
Watching them torment the wicked
Fish in its blue pool.

Случай у паятника Джордано Бруно

Чавкающий белый мяч футбольный
Мне влепил мальчишка в лоб случайно.
Не упав, я молча отвернулась
И увидела костер Джордано Бруно.
Фурии и змеи мне шептали
В миг почти ослепшие глаза:
«Не гуляй там, где святых сжигали.
Многим можно, а иным нельзя»

Этот случай может показаться, да и есть на самом деле, смешным и
нелепым. Но стоить вспомнить Монтеня, который рассказывает о своем
брате Сен Мартене, неожиданно скончавшемся через шесть часов после
того, как мяч случайно ушиб ему голову над правым ухом.

An incident by the statue of Giordano Bruno

An accident – a little boy kicked a white football
And slathering, it fetched me a blow on the brow.
Still upright, I turned without a word
And saw the pyre of Giordano Bruno.
The furies and serpents whispered to me
For a blinding second, my eyes were shut
'Do not walk there, where saints were burned
Many may and yet some may not.'

This incident may appear to be, and in fact was, quite absurd. But it is
worth remembering Montaigne, who told of how his brother San Marten
died without warning, six hours after being hit by a ball above his right ear.

Забастовка элекриков в Риме

В ту ночь на главных площадях
Вдруг электричество погасло.
Луна старалась – только, ах –
Не наливайся так, опасно!

Фонтаны в темноте шуршали,
Но что-то в них надорвалось.
Как будто вместо них крутилась,
Скрипя и плача, мира ось.

И тьма, тревожима Селеной
Чуть трепетала, будто море.
И люди, сливки мглы, качались
Придонной водорослью в бурю.

Тьма нежная и неживая –
Живых и мертвых клей и связь.
Вдруг вечный мрак и вечный город
Облобызались, расходясь

Rome's electricians strike

That night on the main squares
Suddenly all the lights were gone
The moon strained – oh, take care –
Unsafe – you'll blow, don't struggle so –

The fountains whispered on in darkness
But something in them – overtaxed
As if wheeling in their place,
And keening, was the world's axis.

And darkness, stirred by Selene
Like a sea, slightly quivered.
And people – skimmed from twilight's lip
Rocked like flotsam in storm weather.

Lithe and lifeless night
Between living and dead, the link, the paste
The eternal dark, eternal city
Kissed suddenly, went their separate ways

У Пантеона

Площадь, там где Пантеона
Лиловеет круглый бок,
Как гиганта мощный череп,
Как мигреневый висок,
Где мулаты разносили
Розы мокрые и сок –
Там на дельфинят лукавых
Я смотрела и ушла
В сумрак странный Пантеона
Прямо в глубь его чела.

Неба тихое кипенье
В смутном солнце января –
Надо мною голубела
Пантеонова дыра,
Будто голый глаз циклопа
Днем он синий, вечерами
Он туманится, ночами
Звезд толчет седой песок.
Уходила, и у входа
Нищий кутался в платок
А слоненка Бернини
Полдень оседлал, жесток,
Будто гнал его трофеем
На потеху римских зим,
И в мгновенном просветленье
Назвала его благим –
Это равнодушье Рима,
Ко всему, что не есть Рим.

By the Pantheon

On the square where the Pantheon's
Curved flank gleams purple
Like a giant's mighty skull
Like a migraine-pulsed temple
Where juice, damp roses
Are handed out by mulattos –
There I watched the archness
Of dolphins, then left
Into the Pantheon's strange dusk
The dome of its forehead

The quiet simmering of the sky
In a vague January sun –
Blueing above me
The hole of the Pantheon
Like the Cyclops' naked eye
Day's sea-blue, at evening
It mists over, at night
A star grinds the grey sand.
I went out and at the entrance
A beggar wrapped in a blanket
And Bernini's little elephant
Saddled by cruel midday
As if to ride out his trophy
For Roman winter play
Then I saw it was an honour
In a moment it struck home:
It is Rome's indifference
To all that is not Rome.

Сад виллы Медичи

В центре Рима, в центре мира
В тёмном я жила саду.
Ни налево ни направо
Ночью нету на версту
Никого, кроме деревьев
Померанцевых замерзших.
Кроме стаи кипарисов
Саркофагов, тихих статуй.
И стеной Аврелиана
Этот сад был огражден.
Здесь ее ломали готы,
Здесь они врывались в Рим,
То есть это место крови.
И на нем мой дом стоял.

Ночью войдешь –
Никого…а кто-то смотрит.
Тихо вздрогнет половица,
Приотворится окно,
А в глухую полночь дробью
Барабанят стены, пол.
Чуть задремлешь – тут кувалдой
В потолок стучать начнут.

Я привыкла, я привыкла,
Не совсем сошла с ума
Только дара сня благого
Этот дух меня лишил
Хоть бесплотен, но нелегок –
Фердинанд, Атилла, Гоголь?
Или мальчик рядом с домом
Спящий в мраморном надгробье,
Отстраненный и немертвый?
Страшен этот взгляд тяжелый,
Взгляд, текущий не из глаз.

The Garden of the Villa Medici

In the centre of Rome, in the centre of the world
In a dark garden, my home
Nothing, nothing about me
At night for miles around
Apart from trees
Rimy bitter orange trees.
Apart from flocks of cypresses,
Sarcophagi, soundless statues.
And the Aurelian Wall
Kept guard around this garden.
Here the Goths laid wall to waste,
Here they broke and entered Rome,
So this is a place of blood.
Here, where my house stood.

Entering at night –
No one... but someone watches.
A floorboard quivers quietly,
A window pushed ajar,
But come midnight's depths
They drum with clubs on walls and floor.
Let your eyes close, and then
On the ceiling begins the sledgehammer's roar.

I'm used to it, I'm used to it,
I haven't entirely left my mind
Only the gift of healing sleep
Is denied to me by this soul
Fleshless perhaps, and yet not weightless –
Ferdinand, Attila, Gogol?
Or the boy by the house
Who sleeps in a marble sepulchre,
Estranged and undead?
This heavy glance is terrifying,
A glance which weeps not from the eye.

Кто бы ни был дух упорный –
Мелочь сорная иль князь
В ночь последнюю простился –
В ручку двери он вселился –
Ящерицей темной стала,
Быстро нагло побежала
Вверх и вниз.

Я узнала этот ужас –
Тихий, будто первый в жизни
Легкий белоснежный снег.
Так прощай, сад Медичийский,
И стена Аврелиана,
Гоголь, piazza Barberini,
И похожая на колхозницу статуя богини Рима.
Всею душой, подбитой
Белым шелком ужаса, отныне,
Все равно я о вас тоскую.
И о зимних горьких померанцах.

Whoever owned this stubborn soul –
Worthless nobody or prince
Last night he took his leave
Settled on the door latch
Becoming a dark lizard,
It ran rapidly, unflinching
Up and down.

I saw this terror for what it was –
Quiet, like the first light fall
Of white snow in a life.
Farewell, Medici Garden
Farewell, Aurelian Wall,
Gogol, Piazza Barberini
And the statue of Rome, so like a Soviet farmgirl.
With all my soul, lined
With the white silk of terror, henceforth
And in spite of, I will long for you.
And for winter's bitter orange trees.

Из Марло

Безрукие, безносые, слепые,
Глухие и старухи, как деревья
На пустоши чернеющие в мраке,
Все жить хотят. Вот только что младенцы…
Про этих я не помню и не знаю.
Все жить волят. Что за приманка в жизни?
Быть может, мелких радостей набег?
Пробежка солнца по лицу слепому?
Вкус сливы или друга поцелуй?
Иль низменное злое содроганье?
Что держит нас, что нам уйти мешает?
Незнание, неверие в Другое?
Иль просто это – протяженность жизни?
И сладостно-мучительное в нас
Скольжение ее прозрачной лески,
Что чувствуем мы – кончится крючком.
Но пусть скользит и мучит – пусть мгновенье.
Но я – другой, я – птица, я – бродильня,
Пока во мне кристаллы песнопенья
Не растворятся до конца во мраке –
Я петь желаю.

By Marlowe

The blind, those with stumps for arms, holes for noses
The unhearing, the old women, like trees
In a wasteland, black shapes in the murk,
All want to live. Still, perhaps not the babies...
I don't recall – I know nothing of them.
All desirous of life. What is this lure to live?
Could it be the inroad of small pleasures?
The sunlight chasing over a blind face?
The taste of plum or the kiss of a friend?
Or the quivering grasp of miserable rage?
What holds us here, prevents us from departing?
Is it lack of knowledge, lack of belief in Another?
Or is it simply this – the extent of life?
And the slipping-sliding sweetly agonising
Of its transparent line within us,
Ending, we sense, in a hook.
Yet let it slip and slide and agonise – for a moment.
But I am different, I am a bird, I am in ferment
And until the last crystals of my song-singing
Have dissolved in the murk
I will sing.

Освобождение Лисы

По мертвой серебром мерцающей долине,
По снегу твердому,
По крошкам мерзлым
Лиса бежит
На лапах трех.
Четвертая, скукожившись, лежит
Окровавленная в капкане.
Лиса бежит к сияющей вершине,
То падая, то вновь приподнимаясь –
То будто одноногий злой подросток,
То снова зверь больной
На шатких лапах.
Там на вершине ждет ее свобода,
Небесный Петербург,
Родные лица.
Лиса бежит, марая чистый снег,
Чуть подвывая
В ледяное небо.

The Freeing of Fox

Through the dead silver glint of valley
Over the firm snow
Over stiff-frozen flakes
Runs fox
On three paws.
The crumpled fourth lies
Bloodied in a trap.
Fox runs towards the shining summit
Now falling, now picking herself up again
Now a seething one-legged teenager
Now once more a beast in pain
On trembling paws.
There, at the summit, and waiting, her freedom
Heavenly Petersburg,
Familiar faces.
Fox runs, staining the clean snow
Howling gently
At the icy heavens.

На заре

Когда над тазом умывальным
Встает, кровавится восход,
Когда в поход уходит дальний
Воздушный, пышный, ватный флот,
Когда ты плачем погребальным
Встречаешь каждый новый день
И разговариваешь с тенью,
И сам – чуть-чуть плотнее тень,
Тогда, мне кажется – над бором
Встает последняя заря,
Хвост разомкнулся уробора,
Чтоб из избы не вынесть сора
Мир поджигают три царя.

At Dawn

When the risen sun bleeds
Into the wash-pail,
When a fleet of cotton-wool
Cumulus sets sail,
When you greet each day
With graveside despair
And hold forth to a shadow
Though you yourself are barely there,
It seems then that above the copse,
The last dawn unfurls
Uroborus lets his own tail drop
An end to dragging buckets of slops
From the hut: the three kings set light to the world.

Обряд перекрестка

Б. Улановской

На перекрёстке двух дорог
В полях я свечку зажигала,
И на коленях, на снегу,
Стихи безумные читала,

И глядя в гулкое звездилище,
Щепотку слов роняла вверх –
Не для себя, не для себя –
Для Бога, для зимы, для всех.

Слова взлетали будто рыбки
Златые, плавали по небу,
И падали, как будто галька
Иль катышки цветные хлеба.

Ritual at the Crossroads

To B. Ulyanovskaya

At the point where two roads cross
I lit a candle in the snow,
In the fields, on my knees,
I read out mind-less poems.

And glancing at the humming stars
I let a few words fall above
Not for myself, not for myself
For God, for winter, for all of us.

The words flew up like little fish
Golden, swimming in the sky,
And fell, like a pebble falls
Or brightly coloured bread-balls.

Обручение с Фонтанкой

С тобой, поганая река,
Я обручилась будто дож –
Тот перстень в глуби вод бросал,
А я – любимой кошки труп,
Которая со мною рядом спала, дремала
Столько лет,
Мурлыкала, гортанно пела…
В ее глазах любовь
Две маленькие свечки засветила,
Когда она за мной (всегда) следила.
Река лежала как рука
В анатомическом театре,
И синий мускул был разъят
Лучом ланцета неземного.
Вот анатомии уроки
Души, вот Рембрандт мой…
Ты, мусорная, злая и нагая,
Ты водоросли слабо шевелишь,
Вот ты теперь всегда со мною рядом.
Подводных, тусклых глаз не сводишь,
Своим песком глядишь.
И рыбам, и пиявкам всем, и гадам
Со мною разговаривать велишь.

Betrothal to Fontanka

To you, despicable river
I am betrothed, like the Doge
Throwing that ring to the water's depths,
And I am the body of my beloved cat
Who slept by me, slumbered
So many years,
Purred, sung a guttural song...
In her eyes love
Lit two tiny candles,
When she (as always) followed me.
The river lay like a hand
In the dissecting room
And the ray of a heavenly lancet
Cuts bare the blue sinew,
Here lessons in the soul's
Anatomy, here my Rembrandt...
You waste-laden, vicious, naked thing
You barely stir the water-weed,
Now it's you – forever at my side,
Never taking your dim, deepwater eyes off me
Staring with your sand
And fish and leeches and slippery creatures –
You bid them all talk with me.

* * *

В эту Иванову ночь
Так томительно жить!
Нежитью лучше в луче
Над полями кружить.
Лучше бесплотною стать
И в одуванчик войти,
И дуновеньем одним
По ветру себя разнести.

* * *

What torment living is
On this Midsummer's night
Better, to be a dark spirit
And fly over fields in light.
Better to shed all flesh
And enter the dandelion
And with a single breath
Be scattered far and wide.

* * *

Входит Осень. Солнце. Холод
Главное с тропы не сбиться.
Лист упал и посоветовал
Покориться и смириться.

И снова все начнет сбываться,
Хлынет свет в средину лба,
Сигареты умножатся
В твоих карманах как хлеба.

* * *

Autumn comes. The sun. The cold.
Stay on the forest track.
A falling leaf counsels me
Remain humble – do not fight back.

And once again it comes to pass
That sudden light upon my head,
And pocketed cigarettes
Divide – increase, like loaves of bread.

SHIP

Корабль

Из ничего

О погоди!
Скажу! Скажу!
О дай мне миг
Еще один.
Как клавесин,
Стучащий в Рай
И рвущий розу,
Ты мне на времени сыграй
Метаморфозу.
О погоди!
Хоть миг один.
Я и пчела,
Я и цветок,
Не разлучай наш брак,
И в трепете сладимый сок
Ты – храм разрушенный,
И там
Плитой пробился
Колокольчик.
Он службу служит и звенит,
Пока окрестность спит.
О погоди! Скажу! Скажу!
Но я скольжу
В безвидный мрак,
Уже не колокольчик – мак,
Уже не мак, а птица,
Уже не птица – кровь,
Которую пускают всем,
Кто слишком много хочет.
Ужель ты кинешь меня к тем,
Кто колет тень и рубит тень
В скале молчания – к совсем
Немым горнорабочим?

Out of Nothing

Wait!
I'll tell you! I will!
Give me a moment
Just one more.
Like a harpsichord
Tapping at Paradise
Plucking at roses,
Play to me awhile
Of metamorphosis.
Oh please wait!
Just one moment more.
I am both bee
And flower,
Do not set our union asunder,
In the quivering, the sweetest nectar
You are a temple in ruins,
And there
A bluebell breaks through,
Like a headstone,
Jingling, marking Mass,
Whilst the land around sleeps.
Oh wait! I'll tell you, I will!
But I am slipping into
Unseeing black,
Not a bluebell any longer – a poppy,
No longer a poppy, but a bird
No longer a bird – now blood,
Which is let by all those
Who desire too much.
Surely you wouldn't throw me to
The cutters and shovellers of darkness
On the sheer face of silence – the dumb
Utterly dumb miners?

TRANSLATOR'S NOTES

The Christmas Mystery in Kolomna

Vertep is a mystery play or a mummers' play which retells the story of the Nativity, featuring characters such as Herod, the Shepherds, the Three Kings, Death and Satan. It was historically performed by puppets, but is now often acted out instead.

Kolomna is a suburb of St Petersburg

Fontanka is a river in the centre of St Petersburg.

'*...the theatre's greening corpse*': the Bolshoi Dramaticheskii Teatr (BDT) is located on the embankment of the Fontanka river and is traditionally painted green. Elena Shvarts' mother, D.M. Shvarts, was the much respected literary manager of this famous theatre. Elena Shvarts was quoted in the literary journal *Znamya* (no. 4, 2001) as saying that her mother was initially indignant at the unflattering description of her theatre.

'If you and I should think to die...'

'*Goodbye sphinx, goodbye canal...*' A sphinx, excavated from Thebes in 1832, sits on a granite plinth on the embankment outside the Academy of Arts in St Petersburg.

Several canals and small rivers such as the Fontanka cross the centre of the city. For this reason the city is sometimes called the Venice of the North.

'*Goodbye fortress with your bloodless face*': The St Peter and Paul Fortress, a notorious Tsarist prison. The revolutionary Karakozov made an unsuccessful attempt on the life of Alexander II in 1866 and was hanged at the St Peter and Paul Fortress.

'*...Yards and houses of a thousand homes...*': the Russian phrase '*dokhodnye doma*' means literally 'houses of income'. It refers to the monumental blocks of flats built in St Petersburg in the 19th century to cater for a growing urban population. The warren-like flats were rented out, rather than sold, thus ensuring the 'income'.

Memory's Sideways Glance

'*(Temple has two meanings in English)*': In Russian the words for temple on the head and temple as a place or worship are different. This bracketed note is in the Russian original.

'*With your might from Ladoga...*': The Neva flows between Lake Ladoga and the Gulf of Finland.

Poetico – More Geometrico

'*...In the word's corner shrine*': The phrase in Russian means 'red (beautiful / sacred) corner' and it used to refer to the corner of the room where the icon hung. Later it was taken over by the Soviets to mean a corner where 'educative' posters and books were placed.

The Circulation of Time in the Body

'Entre chien et loup': The Russian phrase *'mezhdu sobakoi i volkom'* (*lit.* Between the dog and the wolf) comes from the French and has the same meaning as the French: the twilight time between day and night. I have reverted to the French here to preserve the image.

Mouse

Nevskii: The main street in St Petersburg.

Lucifer Foretold

The epigraph to this poem is not a quotation. The author is addressing Lucifer.

Birdsong on the Seabed

Lampada: The small light which hung over an icon or holy object: an icon-lamp.

March of the Fools on Kiev

(a real happening – see Pryzhov): Ivan Grigor'evich Pryzhov was a 19th-century historian, ethnographer and collector of folktales. He wrote histories of taverns, drunkenness and vodka, and is best known for his book *The Destitute of Holy Rus'*. During his life Pryzhov, a convinced atheist, collected stories about 'fools, false prophets and liars' who operated within the Russian Orthodox Church. Shvarts borrows from Pryzhov the story of a march of Fools in Christ, led by a woman called Matrena. The fate of these pilgrims is unknown. Pryzhov's own fate was unhappy. He was involved in a group led by Nechaev, the revolutionary, and was condemned to hard labour in Siberia in 1871.

Iurodivy is a fool in Christ. There are long traditions of 'Iurodivstvo' in Russian culture and religion. *Iurodivye (pl.)* feigned madness, dressed in rags or went naked. They often spoke in riddles, and they behaved in an eccentric and unconventional manner. They were supposed, though, to possess powers of prophecy and they were respected as clairvoyants and religious figures. It was, for example, accepted for the Tsar to take advice from a *Iurodivy*. Those venerated as *Iurodivye* often included the dispossessed, beggars and wanderers, and sometimes the genuinely insane. Some Russian *Iurodivye* were canonised.

Kiev was the centre of religious life in Holy Rus' until its fall to the Mongols in 1240. The Monastery of the Caves in Kiev was

170

founded in the eleventh century. In this poem it is contrasted with worldly, godless Moscow.

Flora of the Ukraine
Haidamaky: Ukrainian paramilitaries who opposed Polish rule.
Braveheart: Type of mallow (*Malva sylvestris*).
Mova: The Ukrainian word for language.
Hetman: Commander in the Cossack army.
Kanev on the banks of the River Dnieper (where Taras Shevchenko, Ukraine's national poet, is buried).

Grand Elegy on the Fifth Corner of the Earth
'Luke, Matthew, Mark and John': The four gospels are often represented by beasts: Mark is a lion, Luke a bull, John an eagle and Matthew a man or an angel.

An Englishman Roasted in Moscow
Tsar Ivan IV (commonly known as Ivan the Terrible) (1530-84) was notorious for the cruelty of his punishments.

Gogol on the Spanish Steps
'A man with a stoop and a long nose' is an instantly recognisable portrait of the writer Nikolai Gogol, who during the 1840s lived in Rome, where he wrote his famous work *Dead Souls*.
Gogol's name translates as 'golden-eye' – a type of bird.

Piazza of the Knights of Malta
'... poor Pavel / was whipping his hoop along' a reference to Paul I, Emperor of Russia between 1796 and 1801, who was elected Grand Master of the Knights Hospitaller, after the order fled Malta and Napoleon and was established in Russia. Paul I was assassinated.

The Sky in Rome
Lazzaroni, here, street urchins.

By Marlowe
This poem is written as if by Christopher Marlowe.

At Dawn
Uroborus: the ring-shaped symbol of a snake devouring its own tail.

www.ingramcontent.com/pod-product-compliance
Lightning Source LLC
Jackson TN
JSHW011938131224
75386JS00041B/1431

* 9 7 8 1 8 5 2 2 4 7 8 3 6 *